Therefore shall a man leave his father and his mother, and shall cleave unto his wife: and they shall be one flesh.
- Genesis 2:24

BEYOND I DO

Copyright ©2020 Victor Macarthy.
All rights reserved. First paperback edition printed 2020 in the
United Kingdom. A catalogue record for this book
is available from the British Library.
ISBN 978-1-913455-10-1
No part of this book shall be reproduced or transmitted in
any form or by any means, electronic or mechanical, including
photocopying, recording, or by any information retrieval system
without prior written permission of the publisher.
Published by Scribblecity Publications.
Printed in Great Britain.
Although every precaution has been taken in the preparation of this
book, the publisher and author assume no responsibility for errors or
omissions. Neither is any liability assumed for damages resulting from
the use of this information contained herein.
Scripture quotations marked NLT are taken from the
Holy Bible, New Living Translation, copyright © 1996, 2004,
2015 by Tyndale House Foundation. Used by permission
of Tyndale House Publishers, Inc., Carol Stream, Illinois
60188. All rights reserved.

Acknowledgement

The first acknowledgement goes to the One who visited me on a hospital bed in London on 31st December 1989 and gave me an assignment of purpose in life, the one who never gave up on me and still sought me out seven years later to remind me that I had not started His work. To the one who continually renews my strength to serve Him and His purpose in life and Ministry, the One who again saw me faithful (in my unfaithfulness) to give me this assignment of writing this book. He literally dictated the structure of the book. He is my Lord Jesus Christ, without whom I am nothing. I give Him all the praise and honour.

Heartfelt thanks goes to my parents Robert (RIP) and Grace Macarthy whom God used to plant His faith seed in my heart and from whom I learnt resilience and trust in God in times of challenges in life.

My next acknowledgement goes to my church family, Christ Harvest Centre EPC London for their continuous encouragements and support, especially the wonderful couples that the first draft of the book was used as a pre-marriage counselling notes for. Thank you to – Emmanuel and Tracey, Gbenga and Arin, Mark and Flora, Andrei and Karolina, Omar and Marjorie, Luther and Jennifer, Osazuwa and Monioluwa. Your comments, questions and challenges were all considered in producing this book. May God continually strengthen and flourish your relationships and families.

Special thanks goes to my wife, Bola, who spent time, sometimes after a long day at work, reading through drafts and making necessary grammatical corrections, may God continue to bless and increase you in wisdom and strength. I cannot forget Amaka, a mentee, who after reading the first few pages at the start of the book motivated and encouraged me with constant calls and visits to ensure that the work was completed. May God always send you help.

I also thank my sister, Elder Toyin who used her over 30 years of marriage to advise and edit the first draft, may the blessings of God abide with you continually.

Appreciation also goes to Barbara Ifezue and her Scribblecity publication team. Thank you all for your patience and professionalism throughout the process of this publication. You made it easy for me as a rookie author. I pray God's blessings on all you do in life and ministry.

My acknowledgement and appreciation cannot be complete without thanking in advance, my readers, whom God will place this book (hard copy or electronic) in your hands to read about God's heart on relationships. To you, I pray you will find God's wisdom, courage and strength for your relationships and journey of life. May you experience His peace for your heart and rest on all sides. May **Beyond I Do** serve as a catalyst for change and the beginning of a new move of God in your relationships and home.

Amen.

Reviews

Whether you are engaged to be married or have been married for decades, reading the book on 'Beyond I Do' can help you to have a growing, healthy biblical marriage. From understanding God's design for marriage to learning your spouse's love language, to improving communication and remembering what it felt like when you were first together, this book can help you to deepen your love and put God at the centre of your marriage.

Reading this book has helped me to experience a deeper and richer levels of intimacy with my husband by discovering how we each show and receive love. 'Beyond I Do' is as practical as it is insightful. The book reflects the complexities of relationships today, and reveals intrinsic truths, applying relevant, actionable wisdom in ways that work. This is a MUST read book for every couple! Happy reading!

Helen Balogun Ogbemudia
- Cert, Dip, Bsc, Msc, MNSC Accred.

Beyond I Do is an amazing book. Timely, scripture based, with real life examples, easy to read and relevant for those intending to get married and those who are married. A Practical guide to improving marriages - "God wants to bring healing, deliverance, reconciliation and restoration to His people, if only they will take heed!" Each person has to do the needful for victory and continuous joy to be experienced. I wholly recommend this book and pray it will become an instrument in the hands of the Lord to birth love, peace and joy in many homes.

Rev (Dr) & Pastor (Mrs) Jama
Senior Pastors - Good News Assembly UK

Beyond I Do is a book that speaks volumes for itself, more so where it stresses the need for the application of divine order and intent in situations where relations have gone sour or waned. In our present dispensation, God's sacred institution of marriage has become the missing piece of the puzzle. The honey has gone out of most marriages and many need to be illuminated to appreciate the desire to be in this very profound institution of God, even believers.

In our candid opinion, everyone needs this practical manual of Rev. Victor Kenny Macarthy to help boost, bolster and enhance their relationship. We highly recommend this magnificent must read piece.

Rev. Henry and Rev. Mrs.Mensah Bonsu
(Christ the King Dominion Place) UK

Foreword

Victor Kehinde Macarthy; affectionately known as Kenny is the lead pastor of Christ Harvest Church in London. He has a great passion for reaching the lost and for Nigeria, his home nation, and for London, his adopted city and for couples who are about to marry or who are already married.

Kenny has performed a valuable service for the church world wide by bringing wisdom, guidance and sound teaching within the pages of this book. There have been many books written on the subject of marriage over many many years, but within the pages of this work, there are examples and systematic Biblical teaching which are aligned to the every day working out of relationships. His use of clear chapter structure with clever headings will lead every reader deeper into truth and will help each reader to clearly grasp the priorities of good Christian living and good clear moral behaviour.

This book is more than a 'handbook' on marriage it is a wise spiritual perspective from a seasoned leader with a great pastoral heart.

I pray that everyone who reads this book will find their lives enhanced by its teaching and values, it is valuable teaching for those who are new to the faith, and for those who have journeyed with God for many years. It is a privilege for me to write the foreword.

Geoff Feasey
Retired Regional Superintendent
of The Elim Pentecostal Churches

CONTENTS

Acknowledgement	v
Reviews	vii
Foreword	ix
Introduction	1
Carry Overs	10
Covenant	24
Communication	32
Coupling	40
Competing or Controlling?	54
Cash Matters	65
Conflict Resolution Management	85
Communities	119
Children	140
The Final C	150
References	153

1
INTRODUCTION

Sometime ago, the Lord spoke to me on the challenges that his people were facing in having fruitful and rewarding relationships. The message was centred more on marriage relationships, and how the enemy is taking advantage and using unhealthy marriage relationships to affect the end-time assignment of the Kingdom of God.

The Lord gave me some key words beginning with 'C' as the brook-stones to slay the "Goliaths" in our homes (1 Samuel 17), thus bringing restoration and a new beginning to damaged and non-productive relationships. These I will discuss later.

Families that are meant to be battle axes and weapons of

INTRODUCTION

warfare in the hands of God to devastate the kingdom of darkness and establish the will, the counsel and the Kingdom of God, have themselves been held captive like POWs (Prisoners of War). This is the sad situation of many relationship, and God wants to bring healing, deliverance, reconciliation and restoration to His people, if only they will heed to His word.

Like Apostle Peter in Acts 12, the 'Herods' of our days have set their eyes on the marriages and relationships of the people of God and held many bound in the prison walls of life.

Having just carried out an evangelical outreach in a prison, I saw what life behind bars looks like. No matter how spiritual, educated, rich, handsome or pretty you are, when you have the misfortune of being put in a prison; innocent or guilty, your aspirations, plans and actions are curtailed, if not truncated.

Peter was seriously anointed. He was called and discipled by Christ. He was in the upper room to receive the Holy Spirit. He preached a fearless, heart wrenching sermon that saw thousands saved, not once, but several times! He healed the lame man at the Beautiful Gate of the temple. Indeed, his spiritual record was impressive, but once he was imprisoned, his calling and all his ministerial aspirations, plans and actions were brought to a screeching halt.

If you study chapter 12 of Acts of the Apostles, you will see that verses 6 and 11 highlight Peter's situation when he was in prison. The bible says Peter was chained, hand and foot, guarded by sentries (agents of the tyrannical reign of Herod), his garments removed, and sandals taken off his feet. Please, I just don't want you to look at these verses literally, but with deeper spiritual understanding; knowing that the physical is a reflection of the spiritual. Nothing happens in the physical until it has been commissioned from the spiritual realm.

With that understanding, let us look at Apostle Peter's state again; **HANDS** bound. What do hands signify? Aristotle referred to the hand as the "tool of tools." Biblically, the hand(s) has several meanings, but the key ones are strength, power and protection. Also hands can connote generosity, hospitality and

INTRODUCTION

stability such as when we support our brethren. As it is popularly said, we "lend a hand." Sadly, Peter's hands were bound, and he could not exercise strength or power, neither could he be generous or hospitable to anyone – HE WAS IN PRISON, CHAINED.

How about Peter's feet? How did chaining his feet affect him? You've heard the saying: "we go where our feet takes us…" – this in itself is about our lives as a whole. (Psalm 18:33 – 36). Peter's FEET were for spiritual mobility, to go to places Jesus had sent him, but his feet were bound. Apostle Peter had been STOPPED (albeit temporarily) from operating and fulfilling God's purpose.

What was stripped from him? His GARMENT. Does this mean anything to us at all? My question to us in answering this is, what do we use garments for? Simply for COVERING. Generally, this represents authority, dignity, identity, level of prosperity and above all, righteousness. The bible talks about robes of righteousness. Jesus' righteousness covers us as believers to enable us to approach God as our father. There are garments of unrighteousness or filthy garments as in (Zechariah 3: 1-5). These items stripped from Peter are all significant in life and ministry.

The bible teaches that we should put on the whole armour of God in Ephesians 6. In prison, you are stripped of every armour down to the last piece of clothing, and only given a standard prison uniform. In a manner of speaking, the identity the devil and the world would like to know you by is issued to you.

With all these things said, liken Apostle Peter's prison experience to a relationship that has been hijacked by the enemy and put in prison. The parties in the relationship are imprisoned, they have been stripped of their armour and garments of identity, power and righteousness, and they are bound with chains – chains of hatred and disdain towards each other, chains of unforgiveness, selfishness, self-centeredness, pity-partying, chains of hard heartedness and pride toward God, His Word and any voice of reasoning, chains of poverty and lack of breakthrough, to mention a few.

Such people are struggling in every ramification of life – spiritual, family, business, work, children etc, and have become helpless like Peter, and like Peter, all they think they can now do is accept the status-quo and SLEEP. Most people are fast asleep in their relationships. They have given up on the violent and abusive spouse, given up on the drunken, adulterous husband, called it a day on the stubborn, hard hearted and irreverent wife; given up on the selfish, self-centred arrogant spouse always threatening fire and brimstone. They have hung up their fighting gloves for the manipulative spouse; in fact they have given up altogether. They are now going through the motions, waiting for the fire to finally die, as the coals turn to ashes.

In fact, maximising your relationship potential becomes almost impossible, because you have been curtailed. You now live under a yoke of limitation. Sometimes, you may say to yourself defiantly, that you are still gaining some victories, but this is where I need to remind you that even prisoners are fed to be kept alive to serve their terms. No matter the supposed hollow victory you may be claiming, you can never compare it to what could have been if you were free from this prison yard of life. Don't forget the sentries that Peter was chained to so he could not escape. Is a voice in your head or mind deceiving you that you are doing well in prison? That voice is not of God, the Bible says '…where the Spirit of God is, there is liberty…' You can't be in this prison of a sour and unhappy relationship and convince yourself all is well. IT IS NOT! The voice of the sentries are meant to control and keep you in prison until 'Herod' is ready to disgrace and possibly kill your dreams and aspirations and render you useless to the Kingdom of God.

We cannot afford that. You, like Apostle Peter, are appointed, and too anointed to remain in prison. Like Peter, heaven is orchestrating plans for your release. You are leaving the prison behind you, and like Peter, you are putting back on, your garment of identity, strength, power and godly character. You are putting back on your sandals of evangelism and missions, because like Peter, the church has been praying earnestly for you. We need you back on the frontline of God's Army. Heaven is not willing to give up on you yet, and the church can't afford to give up on you as well.…We need all soldiers on the frontline. You are part of the remnants that God is counting on to finish the race and you are equipped to finish well. Your

INTRODUCTION

marriage is one of the many blessings God will be expecting you to use as a weapon to victory.

That is the purpose of this book. Like verses 7-10 of Acts 12, this book is to serve as the angel that slapped Peter awake, brought him light in the cruel Roman dungeon, instructed and supernaturally led him out of the prison gates. This is what I pray this book will do for your relationship, life and ministry:

- **Wake You Up From Your Slumber; no matter how deep**
- **Bring God's Light To Your Situation**
- **Bring A Sense Of Urgency To You**
- **Release You From Your Chains**
- **Instruct & Re-Equip You**
- **Lead You Out Of The Prison To A Fulfilled Life & Ministry**

I pray that as Peter heeded (v8 & 9) to the instructions of the angel, that you will not be wise in your own understanding, but obey God's clarion call to you through this book to leave the prison. I pray that as you obey God's call, your chains will fall off, you will be invigorated with new grace, equipped and empowered to maximise God's grace upon your relationship, life and ministry. The following **C**s of a successful marriage relationship will be examined in subsequent chapters.

1. **C**arry overs

2. **C**omplete in Christ and in yourself. It's not a man or woman that will complete you.

3. **C**ovenant and Christ the Centre of your home (servicing the altar)

4. **C**ommunication, Cooperation and Common Grounds

5. **C**omplement not competing or controlling

6. **C**oupling – Companionship, Intimacy and sex (dangerous if misplaced)

7. **C**urrencies & Coins (Managing your money - Finance and Investments)

8. **C**onflict Resolution Management – preferring one to another

9. **C**ommunities – families and friends

10. **C**hildren

2
CARRY OVERS

"He restoreth my soul" Psalm 23:3a (NLT)

A couple deciding to be in a marriage relationship is like a team of two preparing to climb and conquer a mountain summit. The team must only carry the essentials. They can't afford to put rocks in their individual rucksacks and climb. It will weigh them down, disturb their movement, and likely endanger them and their 'team.' So the first thing is to lose all the rocks in their rucksack before they begin the journey, or once they notice that

they have been carrying rocks that are weighing them down and affecting their progress.

This is what this chapter is about - exploring the way your past - family, childhood, and even adulthood influences how you interact with your spouse now. Most people take into their marriage union, negative spiritual, physical, emotional and financial baggage from their past. This can come in several guises: From generational curses that are not identified and dealt with, to physical abuse from those who had authority over them, to lack of a good marriage model. Others have suffered serious emotional damage from rape to rage, and have kept this unaddressed, hoping that one day, it will go away. However, you will agree it's not that easy to get rid of that chain without seeking help. It's like an unwanted yoke round your neck that you need to break away from and we all need help to do this.

All these 'carry overs' soon begin to show their faces in your marriage, and who gets the brunt of it? Mostly your SPOUSE. The person who is meant to be the closest to you. Why, you ask? Because you expect your spouse to be the one to make you happy. We forget that happiness comes from decisions we make in handling issues in our lives, past and present. You lash out, you react, you keep eerily quiet; sparsely communicating, and this begins to cause friction in your home. You don't have an answer, because the little territory the enemy took years ago, he has turned into a stronghold. The enemy has yoked himself to you, and has decided you will not be released from the pains and the impact of the past incidences of your life. But thank God all strongholds can be retaken.

> **2 Corinthians 10:3-5(NIV) teaches:**
> *"3 For though we live in the world, we do not wage war as the world does. 4 The weapons we fight with are not the weapons of the world. On the contrary, they have divine power to demolish strongholds. 5 We demolish arguments and every pretension that sets itself up against the knowledge of God, and we take captive every thought to make it obedient to Christ."*

So with the help of the Holy Spirit, Christ's Word and counsel, you can DECIDE to take back your sanity. You can reclaim the territories the enemy has taken from you by deciding that enough is enough; and as the children of Israel cried out in Egypt to God, you can do likewise and be set free and see the salvation of our God.

> Perfect love casts out fear we read from the bible - **1 John 4:18** (NIV)
> "There is no fear in love. But perfect love drives out fear, because fear has to do with punishment. The one who fears is not made perfect in love."

Let God's love help you get rid of this Goliath. It's time to seek help, it's time to go and nail the baggage of the past to the Cross. Acknowledge where you are in this, be open and honest to God about it, receive His forgiveness, forgive others, seek help, and be free of the baggage forever.

What am I saying here? I am simply saying that things have happened in our lives that we have refused to thoroughly address. We moved them to the back burner, and left them there; not because we don't want to deal with them, but because of the pains they cause us every time we look closely at them. These issues have grown to become strongholds and giants in our lives. They are controlling our behaviour in the home, and breeding animosity in every little issue with our spouse; and this needs to be challenged and dealt with. Neglecting them should not be an option, as they are bound to destroy things in your life at a later stage. I have seen the danger of this in many counselling sessions with couples: from spouses who were sexually abused when they were young and now find it difficult to relate intimately with their spouse, to those who grew up in physically abusive homes and now only sort out domestic disputes by physically abusing their spouse and children, justifying this by calling it discipline.

These may be extreme cases, but think about the woman who is used to getting everything she wants from men through manipulation and sexual favours. On getting married, she finds it difficult to 'scrape and scrap' for money which results in her having 'friends with benefits,' which nearly ends her marriage, bringing shame to her. Or is it the man who has lived all his life being compared to the neighbours' children, and has become so insecure and socially inept that he will not entertain any form of challenge to his authority by his wife, accept any social visit to his home or allow his wife to further her career if she desires to. Or the man whose wife got a promotion and now earns three times his salary, and he decides to relocate to another city so that she would have to give up the new job. These are just a few examples of how the past (in these cases, of abuse leading to insecurity) can inflict pain on your future if not dealt with.

Brenda's Story

This practical story should help with understanding the dangers of ignoring the subtlety of 'Carry-overs.'

Brenda was a happy girl brought up in a secure home with a professional father and a hard working mother in the quiet town of Harlow. Being the first child, she was literally 'spoilt' and pampered by both parents and family alike. Of course, all the love showered on her translated into academic excellence and a free spirited imaginative girl. She was in a position to be envied by any growing child until her father decided to seek better fortunes back in his home country of Ghana. Brenda's father packed up and travelled to Ghana with her younger brother, leaving Brenda and her mum in Harlow. Her dad who was her world left her. That was her first taste of abandonment and betrayal as she called it.

Her life continued in the safety of Harlow town and she kept achieving good grades after initial setbacks following the relocation of her dad and her brother. Things were to get worse when her mum finished her studies and decided to join her husband back in Ghana where he had now settled.

Brenda had mixed feelings about going to Ghana and leaving her friends, so another spate of emotional turmoil ensued. She was unsettled until she got to Ghana. There, things were to get worse for Brenda. She was registered in a village boarding school in the hope of her learning the local ways quicker. Mistake! Brenda suffered all forms of bullying and abuse for three years until she was taken back home to live and school in the township.

Her move to the township to live with her parents, her brother, and other family members brought untold joy to her. She was settled and doing well in her new school until the expectations of her mum, who used to be kind to her when they were abroad, turned their relationship into an untenable one. In Africa, Brenda quickly learnt that responsibility is assumed from a very early age. She suffered physical and emotional abuse from everyone that was meant to be nice to her; this was compounded by her escaping a near rape incident which devastated her and kept her insular for a very long time.

Trusting anyone became a big problem for Brenda. She saw everyone as guilty until proven innocent. Brenda lived her life like this until she finished her university education and started working, only to face sexual harassments from men old enough to be her father. She started nursing the idea of escaping the trap she found herself in, gathering information that she could use to go back to her beloved Harlow. With a lot of fear and uncertainties, but yet with great determination, Brenda completed the process involved in travelling back to Harlow, and landed at Stanstead Airport. Her trusted aunty was waiting for her, the joy and relief Brenda felt can only be imagined.

Again, abuse seemed not to be far from Brenda. Within six months of her joining her aunt, the wheels came off her joy train. Her trusted aunty and others ganged up against her because she refused to be part of their fraudulent operations.

All of this turned Brenda into someone she was not. She now lied to survive scrutiny, she had become suspicious of everyone, distrustful, insecure and fearful; but even with all of this, the basic pleasantness of Brenda remained with her – albeit somewhat tainted. To most people, all that Brenda went through should not have affected her in the future when she got married and had her own children, but sadly, it did.

Brenda got married to a free-spirited man called Kendrick who was raised with love and affection, being the last and only boy in a family of five children. He trusted everyone in his family – his sisters, mum and dad – they were his life, and he adored and loved them all. He always got everything he wanted, literally; and never lacked anything.

Brenda and Kendrick were like brother and sister during their courting years, everything was going well, and they eventually got married. The problem started when

Brenda started to suspect Kendrick of different wrongs: overspending, affection to others, etc. The lack of trust increased to the point that the relationship began to be toxic and was affecting everyone around them including their young children. By this time, Kendrick who was used to getting what he wanted, was now becoming an angry person. Intimacy was alien to their relationship, mistrust, arguments and fights had become the order of the day. Everything that could go wrong in a marriage was basically happening. Their breakthrough came when a friend suggested counselling.

They both agreed and started attending a counselling session being run by an elderly couple. It was during one of these sessions that the issue of "carry over" was discussed. Brenda and Kendrick opened up to the counsellors, and they saw what their unaddressed past lives were doing to their home and marriage. There was a lot of soul searching, crying, forgiving and healing of their heart and home. Kendrick and Brenda are on the mission field abroad serving God together now.

This is a true-life story and there are many Brendas and Kendricks that may need to come to terms with their buried past. There is a popular adage in Africa that says, "The leg of the hurriedly buried corpse is now showing for all to see." A proper burial of the past may be required for some couples with or without counselling. It's time to dig up, reset, bury and seal up the past, and to be healed from it all through God's power of cleansing and forgiveness.

I have heard some people quote, *"God has put all my sins and my past in the sea of forgetfulness."* (**Micah 7:19**) That is true, but the problem is that you are constantly going back to that sea to fish it out because you have not fully dealt with it; and believe it or not, it is affecting one aspect of your life and relationship or the other.

You have chosen to put it on 'low-heat' and send it to the back burner, but you should have thrown the 'burnt food' away – it's no longer good for consumption. Save your 'gas' (energy, effort and emotions) from slowly casseroling the spoilt meal of the bitter past of your life. Turn off the gas, throw the food away and wash-up!

It's time to come clean; face the monster as David faced Goliath, and deal with the past once and for all.

Purposefully, prayerfully, and permanently.

Practical Tips for dealing with your past

1. Acknowledge the impact the ugly past is having on you, your relationship and your home.

2. Make a conscious decision to deal with the past and let it go. Nothing happens except we make it happen – decide to break the stranglehold the past has on you.

3. A problem shared is a problem halved – it's time to bring the past into the open. Talk to a trusted and experienced friend or counsellor; remove the power that secrecy gives to that past incident, and "expose the unfruitful works of darkness" by expressing your pain including your contribution and responsibility for it.

4. The past has victimised you enough. Your past is bullying you. You are scared of it. It

has chained and limited you, and it's time to get angry and stop being the victim. The day you confront a bully is the last day of his power and the first day of your freedom.

5. To gain back control of your life, you have to stop blaming others for the position you find yourself in. Take responsibility and take action - set up a 'war cabinet' against your past – after all it is you that the past is dealing with, others have long moved on.

6. Focus on the present and fight for your bright future. Allowing the past to impinge on your present and distort your future is not wise. Learn from the experience of the past, but focus on the here and now, and fight for your tomorrow.

7. Forgiveness is the key to the prison gate. To not forgive oneself and others is like staying in prison and having the keys to release oneself, but not using it. No matter what may have happened in the past, learn

from it, forgive yourself if you contributed to it, but more than anything else, forgive those who have offended you. That is the key to releasing yourself from the chains of the past.

Trust me, everyone has a past either good or bad; but if it is affecting you adversely now or may affect your future, you must do something about it. Set yourself free from the past. I will close this chapter with a quote I stumbled on recently.

> **"Freedom is what you do with what's been done to you." ~Jean Paul Sartre**

It's time to free yourself from the past which keeps affecting your today.

3
COVENANT

A Modern Day Prenup

In this chapter, I will explore the difference between marriage based on legal contract and marriage based on the true covenant with God. God is the author of marriage . He knows the reason he instituted the first marriage between Adam and Eve in Genesis 2. One of the key reasons we see in Genesis 2:18 is that of perfect companionship - The LORD God said, "*It is not good for the man to be alone. I will make a helper suitable for him.*" God is interested in our well-being that is why he instituted marriage. After the fall of man, sin and destruction came in; which included men tweaking the God made institution of marriage to suit their own lust, greed and selfishness.

I hear some people refer to marriage as a contract

between two people. As much as this is right from a legal perspective, it's only partially right from a God-centred perspective. A godly marriage is not only a contract, but a covenant between God and man (the male and the female) that should not be broken as there are consequences.

Marriage is a God ordained institution. It is not man-made (Gen. 2:24-25, Matthew 19:5; Eph. 5:31) and we should treat it as such. It is meant to be sacred and purposeful. A mere look at the definition of Contract vs Covenant even from a secular English Dictionary will reveal some of these truths.

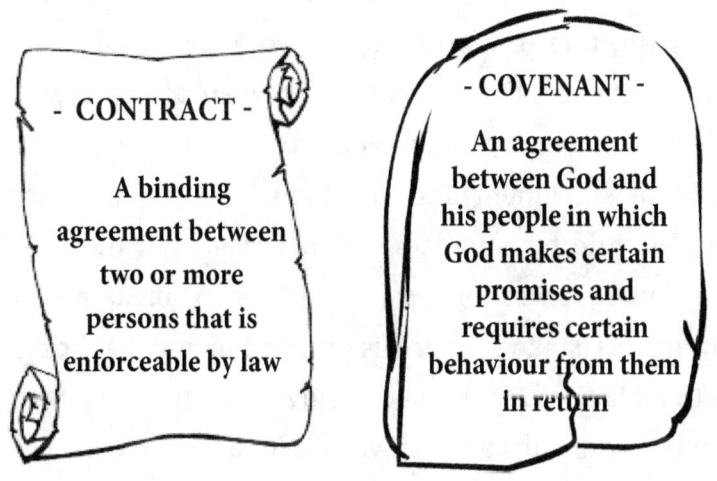

God is the third person in your marriage. If you go via the contract definition route, you can only be dealt with by law if you break the contract; but then, the law has already provided divorce as a means of resolution. This is the limitation of the law. If you are not happy, you can seek divorce, the law will back you up, and you will still be operating legally. It is currently being debated that marriage dissolution should no longer carry a fault (the no-fault divorce) in other words, to eliminate the need for any reason to dissolve and walk out from a marriage. So, to divorce and leave a marriage is becoming easier within the legal frameworks.

If on the other hand you see your marriage as a covenant, then the arbitrator of your marriage is not the law, it is GOD, the creator of heaven and earth; the one who brought you and your spouse to a purposeful place of agreement and covenant. He has attached purpose and blessings to your marriage, but there are also consequences for disobedience or for breaking the covenant. Thank God for His love and mercy that brings us to a place of repentance, forgiveness and love. So if you have only always seen your marriage as a contract, it's time to see it for what it is - a covenant between you, your spouse and God as in Eccl. 4:12b – 'a threefold cord is not quickly broken'.

This simple paradigm shift has a way of changing the way we think, speak and act in our relationship. Give your marriage a new name by redefining and repositioning it with God and for God's purposed greatness for you. It's time to come to the place of the Cross to repent and re-fire. This is wise, as it honours God, and this wisdom helps us to know what and how to speak, think and act in our union.

The place of the marriage covenant is a place of purpose, a place of provision, protection, preservation, pardon (forgiveness and mercy) and peace, as we seek to ensure His will on earth and more importantly in our marriages.

The covenant is a place of agreement, it is a place of grace, a place of favour, a place of guidance and a place of fruitfulness and power. In short, it is a place of dominion.

Where is this place? It's the altar we must create as a

couple to meet God, so that He can continually 'breathe life' upon our marriage and home. This is the place we receive instruction and grace to love and submit. It is also a place we receive his rod of correction, rebuke and restoration.

The Family Altar
– A Place of Family Solution and Power

Once a couple has acknowledged that their union is not only contractual in nature but covenantal with God and their spouse, their next step is to ensure that God through Christ Jesus and the power of His Spirit, becomes the centre of their home. They must give God the presiding right in their hearts, home and life. This is done at the family altar, the agreed meeting place with God as a couple and a family. Remember, God always came down to Adam and Eve in the cool of the day to have fellowship with them; so also, should we have a place where the Lord has fellowship with our family consistently.

Altars, are places where the spiritual and divine meets with humanity, and the supernatural happens.

Instructions, guidance and blessings from God are triggered at the altar. Altars thus carry the presence of a deity, in our case, they carry the presence of God.

People come to altars to honour the presence of deity and to seek solutions to challenges of life or receive blessings. Altars attract sacrifices; in our case, a sacrifice of praise.

The blessings accruing from altars can be reinforced with the story of Obededom in the bible. Here, we see David refusing to bring the Ark of God to his place after seeing a priest struck dead for touching it, but the same Ark became a blessing to Obededom's household where King David placed it, carrying the presence of God in the house of Obededom (2 Samuel 6:9-11). What was God saying here?

Our heart and our homes should always be a place that honours and carries the presence of God. We must make Christ the centre of our heart and our home. He must take over the throne (Gal 2:20; Gen 18:19) by our own choice. God will never force us to serve or honour Him. He could have made us as robots if he wanted to control us that way, but God created us with free will so we can make our own choices and live with the consequences.

I always encourage couples to set up an 'altar' in their home – a dedicated place where they come to meet with God every day. If you do not have such a place or you have not set aside times to meet with God jointly in prayer, please reconsider your ways and set up an altar of covenant in your home. There are many benefits that you stand to gain from this. One is handing the legacy of worship and prayer down to your children – the next generation.

Remember, children have the tendency to do what you do, rather than what you say; so in training them, let them grow up knowing and seeing you pray to the God their parents introduced to them, at the altar of their home.

The busyness of our world and the tricks of the enemy will fight against you setting apart a place and time for God daily in your family and marriage, but this is where you have to 'fight the good fight of faith' to establish an altar unto the Lord in your home.

The family altar should be a place of 'listening and learning' – listening to the Word and the heart of God, learning from His Word on how we ought to represent Him in all life's journeys.

Family altar time is a time of THANKSGIVING, PRAISE, WORSHIP AND PRAYER – Thanking God for His goodness, surrendering all to Him in worship, and praising Him for what He has done and will yet do. It is a time of prayer and supplication to God concerning the family, home, work, health, school, city and nation.

God wants to make your heart and home his residence, but the choice is yours. As Joshua said, choose you this day… but as for me and my house we shall serve the Lord. Joshua 24:14-15.

Enthrone the Lord in your heart, your family and your home.

4
COMMUNICATION

"Communication works for those who work at it." - John Powell

Communication is one of the most vital weapons against the wiles of the enemy in your home. Some people are great communicators while others are not, but as I say to too many counselees, all skills can be learnt, if you are determined and committed enough to make the effort. The bible teaches in Amos 3:3, that there must be agreement before two can walk together. Before we go further here, let us understand the meaning of communication. The English dictionary defines communication as: '...*the activity of communicating; the activity of conveying information*'.

Please note the emphasis I gave to the word 'activity' which in itself means 'any specific behaviour.' With this, I need to add here early, that not all communications is verbal or written. Most of us limit communication to these two, but they are not the only ones.

Can you Stop Talking! I am trying to read!

NON-VERBAL communication is as important as the verbal and the written.

With my pastoral experience, I have had the opportunity to listen to couples, and I sometimes find that some important facts can be concealed in non-verbal gestures which a spouse can use deliberately. The spouse may not fully understand, but don't forget, God is the third person in your tripod of covenant union.

A good example of this was when Sarah laughed at the news that she would give birth in her old age; and justifiably so you may say at 95years. She laughed to herself, but that laughter communicated a fact – UNBELIEF! Unfortunately for her, that non-verbal act was heard by God and it was duly addressed.

> **Gen 18:12-15**
> *"[12] So Sarah laughed to herself as she thought, "After I am worn out and my lord is old, will I now have this pleasure?"*
> *[13] Then the Lord said to Abraham, "Why did Sarah laugh and say, 'Will I really have a child, now that I am old?' [14] Is anything too hard for the Lord? I will return to you at the appointed time next year, and Sarah will have a son."*
> *[15] Sarah was afraid, so she lied and said, "I did not laugh." But he said, "Yes, you did laugh."*

Of course, we all know how that ended. She gave birth a year later to a covenant son, Isaac. Are you like Sarah, hiding under the temporal 'safety' of nonverbal communication? Maybe it's time to communicate openly to God, your spouse and yourself and start living without fear, embarrassment, shame or whatever negative emotion the enemy has chained you to. It is time for you to break free.

Thank God, Sarah's case ended in praise and testimony. Imagine if the non-verbal communication had triggered dangerous and destructive emotions that stir the person to begin to manipulate, control, and connive situations to gain advantage. The result would be damaging to the person and the family. This can unleash the spirit of Jezebel and we know the danger that this can bring to any relationship. The danger of not communicating truthfully, honestly and with a heart of love and readiness to see God glorified in the situation cannot be over-emphasised.

There Are Spouses Who Will Choose Not To Have An Honest And Open Communication, Not Because They Don't Want To Communicate, But Simply Because Of The Way The Other Spouse Reacted To Their Initial Attempt At Honest Communication.

To this group, may I encourage you to not let your spouse's reaction of manipulation or control stop you from doing what is right. "Two wrongs do not make a right." Your spouse's reaction of manipulation, control, put down remarks and the rest of it are wrong as you know, but why allow the enemy to win in your home?

The spirit that is causing your spouse to react negatively is the enemy and it needs to be rebuked and cast out in prayers. You must let your spouse know that their negative reaction is not helping communication in the home. Keeping quiet, while your head and heart are not quiet is a wrong way of reacting. Be bold, be strong, for the lord your God is with you. Arise and shine and invite your spouse to the place of communication in love, respect and honour. DO NOT KEEP QUIET. That is what the enemy wants you to do, to wave the white flag of SURRENDER, while he continues to harden your spouse's heart by letting him or her think they are 'stronger' and winning, (while on the contrary) they are pushing the union to a place of destruction. You know this is the truth, because you have a lot to say, but you are holding it back because of your spouse's perceived reaction. You also know that it's a 'drip, drip' situation, and one day, the bucket will be full and overflow in a flood of problems. That happens when you keep quiet when you should have spoken.

I have used and included some of the words of A. Martelli – a popular writer on effective communication, and highlighted below characteristics of good communication. I will encourage you to adopt these when communicating to your spouse from now, considering that God himself sees communication as vital hence Isaiah 1:18 ...come and let us reason together...! Communication is a two way process – you have to have completed the processes to be sure you have communicated to your spouse well. Do not give advantage to the enemy!

Characteristics of effective communication:

Completeness - Communication should include all the information the recipient needs to evaluate its content, solve a problem or make a decision. It will not benefit anyone if you are withholding some facts and figures with the hope that decision will swing your way – it may, but it's a matter of time before the house built on the sand totally crumbles... and you are to be blamed for withholding information.

Conciseness - Conciseness is not about keeping the message short, but rather about keeping it to a point.

This is the deliberate removal of 'red-erring' – there are information that has no relevance to the decision making of your spouse on the matter you are presenting – safe time and avoid confusing your spouse and remove such from discussion;

Consideration - A sender should always consider and value the recipient's needs, moods and points of view – use examples that the receiver can relate with where necessary. There is no point presenting an important matter in an atmosphere where you know it might not be received well – if it is not a 'life and death' matter – find a conducive time to communicate… at the end of the day you want the information you are communicating to be reasoned and considered thoroughly – so give yourself the best chance possible by finding the right time, place and moment to communicate your information.

Concreteness – For communication to be effective, the message should be supported by facts and figures where necessary and possible.

Courtesy – This is simply to respect your spouse's culture, values and beliefs – you can't bully your way to agreement – or you would soon find out there was no agreement!

Conduciveness - I am looking at this from timing and atmospheric perspectives – is it a good time and are you in a good place to pass across what you consider as an important information to build your home? Learn to pick the right time and place – I encourage couples to set time to discuss important family matters and each to make the booked time… it shows you respect each other and you both see the importance of your relationship and task of building a godly family!

Clearness - Effective, communication has also to be clear and specific. To achieve clearness, the message should focus on a single objective, thus emphasising its importance and catering for a prompt understanding of its contents.

Correctness – Be sure facts are correct and in no way misleading – use all means to ensure that you are passing across correct information. Some spouses deliberately hold material facts when communicating and they expect decisions that would not lead to future problems. I see this as deception and control and should be avoided at all cost. The information you have should be the same your partner has for agreement and effective decision making.

5
COUPLING

Companionship, Intimacy and Sex

This is one of the most important aspects of married life, but at the same time, one of the most ill-addressed, even in the church. The words sex and intimacy come across as taboo among some cultures, and in some churches, and because of this, the enemy is having a field day with such churches or communities. Hardly will you hear a Sunday sermon based on this topic, but we all need to understand the importance of this God-given 'grace' so we do not misuse or misplace it.

I once was in a counselling session with a gentleman and another pastor, and as soon as our counselee mentioned an aspect of his sexual life with his wife, this other counsellor literarily shut him down and said that we could not get involved with that. Personally, I was disappointed. This was someone who trusted us to the point of sharing his life, his finances, career, habits and so much else with us, but as soon as he mentioned **sex**, he was shut down. As I was a junior member of the counselling team, I had to go with this incorrect decision, but later challenged this with my co-counsellor. I give this example to show our so called Christian attitude toward sex and sexual matters.

We need to know that God created sexual intimacy. God, through His Word, gives us very clear guidance on how we can best experience the gift of intimacy and love that He gave us through sex. Sex was given by God as a wonderful experience between husband and wife to provide physical, emotional and spiritual bonding.

The 'rules' guiding sexual intimacy were written by Apostle Paul in 1 Corinthians 6 & 7:
Sexual activities are only permitted within the confines of marriage. Pre-marital sex is, as the bible makes it plain, a sin and so is sex outside marriage by a married spouse. These are known as fornication and adultery respectively. Christians should avoid any form of sexual immorality.

This book is not written to teach sex as a topic. There are many Christian books that have treated this, and if you are having challenges in this area, you are encouraged to do a contextual study of the word 'sex' in the bible or get one of the good Christian books on marriage. Authors such as Myles Monroe and Chuck Swindoll are highly recommended.

Having said this, the points below should be considered in handling intimacy and sex in a marriage.

1 Beyond the Physical:

Sex in marriage is a good thing. From Paul's teaching, apart from the physical act of intercourse, it also involves the emotions and it's a spiritual thing.

However, the way men handle sexual matters differs from the way women process and deal with it. To most men, sex is only a physical act, and so they handle it in that manner. Men respond to the visual, that is what they see. They may see their wife dressed well and looking good, and it triggers their sexual urge. It now becomes a case of I want sex and I have to have sex; which drives them to making a demand even at those times when it is not conducive for their spouse. To this group of men, sex is just a desired activity that has to be carried out. What is the big deal, they may say. It doesn't take much to trigger the sexual urge in men – the dress, the sultry look, the shape, the size, the beauty, all contribute, and all are physically induced.

To most women, it is far more than just a physical action. There is a process to getting to the place of the physical sexual act. A woman's emotions will contribute to determining if she will be interested in the physical act of sex or not. We have learnt over the years that women respond more to what and how they hear words; so screaming, shouting and harassing a woman will definitely not put her in the mood for any sexual act. In contrast, consideration, concern, care and compassion, applied through gentle spoken words throughout the day may well be more productive to bringing her to a place of sexual desire. To a woman, the process leading to sexual contact can be likened to boiling an egg. It takes longer than frying an egg, which is what I will liken to the process for men. Women respond to the gentle words, the gentle touches, little gifts now and then that show care, concern and love, while men respond to the physical – looks, dress, shape, and smell.

If as a man you feel you are not satisfied with the way sex and intimacy is handled in your home, then I will advise you to honestly, before God, and being truthful to yourself, review the way you have been handling your wife in this area in the light of the above.

Do you genuinely love and care for your wife? Are you being gentle with your wife in words and deeds? Do you speak gently and honourably to her? Do you give those little inducing gifts? Do you help her and care for her and show concern for her and her wellbeing to the point that she knows and acknowledges these efforts and sacrifices? If not, you need a wholescale cultural change in this area – and the earlier you carry this out, the better for you, your marriage and your home.

I am assuming here that I am writing to God-fearing men who are not physically or emotionally abusive toward their spouses. If you happen to be a man that physically or emotionally abuses his spouse and still wants and gets sex when you want it, may I say here and now that you are only a bully who is only getting what you want through fear and intimidation, and not out of respect, honour and being wanted. For such a 'boy,' you need to repent, go and truly seek your wife's forgiveness and change before you lose the best gift God has given you besides Jesus and the Holy spirit. You need to become a man and stop being a boy. You need help and you need to seek that help fast, through counsel, advice and deliverance prayers.

Likewise, if as a woman you feel neglected at home in the area of sex and intimacy, you may also have to carry out an honest review of your actions or non-actions in this area.

In all honesty to God and yourself, do you actually respect and honour your husband? Do you make yourself attractive to your husband in the way you present yourself in the home? Do you dress well, look good? Do you make an effort to ensure that you are an object of desire to your husband? Do you make yourself truly beautiful for him? Do you really prepare yourself for your husband when he is coming home? Or do you just go with your cooking clothes to the bed, smelling of oil and cooking spices? Then the fault may be yours to correct; you may need a wholescale culture change.

Remember, in Proverbs, we are told of 'strange women' who travel to far countries to buy spices with the aim of luring their target; and their effort is not noble, but is meant to drag their victim to an early death and destruction through illicit sexual encounters. They travel to buy the best perfumes and present themselves beautifully to their male target. They understand that the men will be aroused by their beauty, looks, shape and smell. They invest their time, money and effort to get their target.

As a wife, you may have to do more than you are currently doing. You may have to invest more time, money and effort into looking good for your husband – not forgetting the standard requirement of respecting and honouring him in your words and actions.

I will complete this point by saying the above advice given to men is equally good for the women to follow. By this, I mean that women should also seek to treat their spouse with love and care and must not be aggressive or violent, showing their appreciation and love with occasional gifts. The man likewise has to take care of his appearance and hygiene.

2 **Maturity in the Bedroom:** Avoid politicising intimacy in the home: I have seen some couples turn sex and intimacy into politics or bargaining chips. We must be mature in handling this aspect of married life, or it can lead to more problems than anticipated. Everything in a marriage relationship must stem from covenant and the fear of God.

I recently read an article that stated that an average man will require sex at least four times a week, that is 16 times in a month. To be honest, I don't know how this research was conducted, but just for the sake of making a point, this statistic shows a huge need for sexual contact by men. I am hoping the number for women will not be far behind if not more. If there is a need for regular sexual contact to have a healthy relationship, then we have to treat sex as the bible teaches it – don't deprive your spouse of sexual contact except during a brief period of spiritual exercise of waiting on God.

I once met a couple, and it later transpired that their sex life was non-existent. They had sex quarterly, that is once every three months, and that was at its most regular, as there had been instances when the man said they had gone a whole year without sexual contact. I had to let them know that this was not healthy for a marriage less than seven years old. I was not surprised that they both humbly sought counsel, as this is a red flag that indicates problems in any marriage.

During the counselling sessions, it transpired that the lady said she'd never liked sex, and only did it just to please the man. Further investigations revealed that her dislike for intimacy or sex came from her experience of sexual abuse in her teenage years. Does this sound familiar? UNRESOLVED CARRY OVERS – those rocks in the rucksack!

She honestly declared that she regularly devised ways of getting out of engaging in sexual contact by faking periods, tiredness, work pressure and that even any negligible wrong action of the husband during the day, she would use as an excuse to avoid sex for a few more weeks. She said she was tempted many times to share her feelings with her husband, but she was scared she would be rejected by him, as she saw him as not understanding her, since he always got upset and angry with her.

On hearing this, I didn't know who to feel sorry for – the man who happens to be a church elder, or the woman, who is an active church worker and who had been carrying such a huge burden for years.

Initially, I saw her action as wicked and uncaring, something that could have led to a broken home, but that was until she was able to share her inner pain.
I asked how she was able to carry on living with such pain for so long, and what she expected her husband to do. She said she was too hurt to care anymore, and she was ready to deal with any consequences, even the loss of her marriage and home.

It was one of the worst cases of unresolved 'carry overs' I have encountered, and it has impacted on that home adversely. She confessed that she played on the fact that as a church elder, the man could do nothing about the situation, and any wrong sexual move would be met with church discipline.

There are women like that out there, who knowingly

or unknowingly use sex as a weapon, and I encourage them to follow the lead of this woman by reviewing their actions in the light of God's word, and make wholesome changes through counsel and prayer.

This story recounted above is not unique to women. There are men that due to their need for sex, arm themselves with that verse of scripture: The body of the man is the woman's and the body of the woman is the man's. They become unreasonable to the point of physically forcing themselves on their wife, in other words, rape.

I have had to intervene in a case like this, where the demand for daily sex became a burden for the wife, and when she asked for time out, it resulted in physical abuse and rape. It became so bad that the woman was just seeking confirmation from anyone to encourage her to run away from her matrimonial home where she already had four children, who were all graduates.

Again, it took long counselling hours with spiritual parents to bring reconciliation and peace.

I leave you with the following passages to ponder on as they relate to intimacy in marriage.

Proverbs 5:15-19

[15] Drink water from your own cistern, running water from your own well. [16] Should your springs overflow in the streets, your streams of water in the public squares? [17] Let them be yours alone, never to be shared with strangers. [18] May your fountain be blessed, and may you rejoice in the wife of your youth. [19] A loving doe, a graceful deer— may her breasts satisfy you always, may you ever be intoxicated with her love.

Song of Songs 7:6-12

[6] How beautiful you are and how pleasing, my love, with your delights! [7] Your stature is like that of the palm, and your breasts like clusters of fruit. [8] I said, "I will climb the palm tree; I will take hold of its fruit." May your breasts be like clusters of grapes on the vine, the fragrance of your breath like

apples, [9] *and your mouth like the best wine. May the wine go straight to my beloved, flowing gently over lips and teeth. 10 I belong to my beloved, and his desire is for me. 11 Come, my beloved, let us go to the countryside, let us spend the night in the villages. 12 Let us go early to the vineyards to see if the vines have budded, if their blossoms have opened, and if the pomegranates are in bloom— there I will give you my love.*

6
COMPETING OR CONTROLLING?

"Competition creates better products; alliances create better companies." - Brian Graham

One of the subtle ways in which couples play into the hands of the enemy to destroy their homes is when they begin to compete with each other. This is one area couples need to come to terms with. They have to critically look inward and face the fact of what they see. I have seen couples compete to the point of ruining their finances and invariably their home. Competition comes in many guises, from career aspirations to gaining the love and support of others, especially their children, to caring for their wider families. Competition can be healthy in some circumstances, but extremely destructive in most areas in the home.

The English Dictionary defines competition as:

"The activity or condition of striving to gain or win something by defeating or establishing superiority over others."

"An event or contest in which people take part in order to establish superiority or supremacy in a particular area."

"The person or people over whom one is attempting to establish one's supremacy or superiority; the opposition."

Looking at these three variants of the definition of competition, it is clear, especially looking at the text in bold, that competition in a home outside playing games or challenging each other to improve spiritually or physically can be destructive.

The first few things worth noting in these definitions of competition are that competition involves:

- *ACTION,*
- *DETERMINATION,*

- ***CREATES AN ATMOSPHERE*** (healthy or not) which leads to:
- ***END GAME*** (a somewhat selfish objective to be accomplished)

The whole objective of competing is to prove supremacy and superiority or win something from someone you have knowingly or unknowingly classified as the opposition. The word 'defeat' in the first definition, brings this out more. Your objective is to plan, strategise and execute to DEFEAT your opponent, in this case, YOUR SPOUSE. Is this not an oxymoron? LOVE that leads to civil war or defeat! This is not an atmosphere that should exist in a godly home because it clearly contradicts God's purpose for marriage and the character of love.

As I was further researching this issue of competition among couples, I stumbled on an article written by someone who is simply called Muse. This article further confirms the characteristics of competition in any relationship thus, and I quote, (bold emphasis is mine):

"Competition is often related to the ***measure of disparity*** between *self-worth* and the *worth of your partner* as *perceived by you*".

The competitive spirit is triggered by the way a spouse PERCEIVES their SELF-WORTH as compared (DISPARITY) to that of their partner's self-worth.
This already tells me that the competing spouse is seeing himself or herself as a DIFFERENT INDIVIDUAL in the relationship. Different in terms of values, aspirations, economics, social life and whatever else. Immediately we perceive differences, competition designed to prove superiority steps in.

Muse further wrote that based on the perceived disparity and self-worth we can arrive at the following different types of couples:

- Both feel successful as well as superior to their partner. (I'm great and I'm better than my partner!)
- Both feel successful, but one partner perceives him/herself as superior to the other partner.
- Both feel successful yet inferior/look up to their partner. (I'm great and you're awesome!)
- One of them feels unsuccessful but despite this,

both of them feel themselves to be superior to their partner.

- One of them feels unsuccessful and one of them feels superior to the other (could be the one who feels successful or the one who doesn't).

- One of them feels successful but both of them look up to their partner (or feel inferior).

- Both feel unsuccessful and yet they look down on their partner. (I'm a loser but you're far worse!)

- Both feel unsuccessful, but one of them looks up to the other while the other doesn't.

- Both feel unsuccessful and look up to/feel inferior to their partner. (I'm a loser but you're not!)

The understanding of couples on how they respond to these two key things: SELF-WORTH and DISPARITY both negatively and positively will go a long way in correcting the competitive behaviour in the relationship. Each spouse must understand that competition stems from those two key issues.

Everyone should understand that God created them uniquely. Even our right thumb print is different from our left. Everyone of the over seven billion people on earth has different iris patterns. That's uniqueness! Couples must understand that although they have different physical and emotional attributes, they are still one before God in purpose. So the key is using our differences to maximise God's purposes in our home and marriage.

> Genesis 2:18 (NIV) shows one of the intentions of God in establishing marriage –
>
> [18] *The Lord God said, "It is not good for the man to be alone. I will make a helper suitable for him."*

God in this verse is not thinking of a competing couple in a marriage relationship but a complementing couple.

Eve was meant to complement Adam. Whatever he lacked, Eve had it.

Also, Genesis 2:24-25 Version (NRSV) reads:

> [24] *Therefore a man leaves his father and his mother and clings to his wife, and they become one flesh. 25 And the man and his wife were both naked, and were not ashamed.*

God's intention and objective here is a unifying of

two people into one individual. One person cannot compete with him or herself. A person can improve from where he or she is, but cannot compete with himself. There must be opposition in a competition. The idea of opposition in a marriage is totally abhorrent. The mindset in a marriage or relationship should always be a mindset of complementing.

The issue of gaining superiority or supremacy should not and must not arise. You need someone else to compare with or to prove superiority to, not

yourself, because marriage makes couples, not two but one. Competition is contrary to God's intention for marriage.

Some may say, but the bible says "the husband is the head..." YES, that is true, but this is a role God has asked husbands to occupy in the marriage relationship, with great responsibility. The wife in a marriage relationship equally has a role to occupy for God and that also comes with great responsibility.

Ephesians 5:21-33 clearly defines the role of the husband and the role of the wife, and nowhere is there room in that passage for competition.

> [21] *Submit to one another out of reverence for Christ.*
>
> [22] *Wives, submit yourselves to your own husbands as you do to the Lord.* [23] *For the husband is the head of the wife as Christ is the head of the church, his body, of which he is the Savior.* [24] *Now as the church submits to Christ, so also wives should submit to their husbands in everything.*

²⁵ *Husbands, love your wives, just as Christ loved the church and gave himself up for her* ²⁶ *to make her holy, cleansing[b] her by the washing with water through the word,* ²⁷ *and to present her to himself as a radiant church, without stain or wrinkle or any other blemish, but holy and blameless.* ²⁸ *In this same way, husbands ought to love their wives as their own bodies. He who loves his wife loves himself.* ²⁹ *After all, no one ever hated their own body, but they feed and care for their body, just as Christ does the church—* ³⁰ *for we are members of his body.* ³¹ *"For this reason a man will leave his father and mother and be united to his wife, and the two will become one flesh."[c]* ³² *This is a profound mystery—but I am talking about Christ and the church.* ³³ *However, each one of you also must love his wife as he loves himself, and the wife must respect her husband.*

The roles, duties and responsibilities start in vs 21:
²¹ *Submit to one another out of reverence for Christ.*

In carrying out our roles and responsibilities to the

marriage union and in our homes, we must consider and where necessary, submit to one another because of our respect, love and reverence for our Lord Jesus Christ and all He represents to us – SAVIOUR, LORD, and SOON COMING KING.

As subtle as the issue of competing may appear, it is a real and present danger among couples and families. The competitive spirit is quite destructive to a home if misplaced.

Muse concluded his article by summarising that "Couples vary in terms of how they perceive themselves, how they measure their success in relation to that of their partner and how they respond to such a judgement (which depends heavily on their personality characteristics). Furthermore, fuzziness in valuation of self and that of the other, will add further complexity. (For instance, a person with a limited understanding of his partner's profession might be ill-equipped to valuate her success). In general, too much of perceived disparity might be detrimental to their relationship with either one or both developing either inferiority complex or superiority complex). The ideal scenario, in my opinion, is when both of them feel successful and yet look up to their partners because they perceive them to be better human beings. Whether this cultivates competition or not is debatable."

I believe couples experiencing the negative impact of competing should start from renewing the mind, unlearning unhealthy habits and behaviours and learning to see their marriage union the way God has set it up – two people becoming one in purpose, achieving God's purpose on earth through their home and family.

7
CASH MATTERS

Currencies & Coins (Managing your money - Finance and Investments)

Money and finance related matters rank high as causes of problems among couples. The Bible teaches that 'money answers all things…' and the same bible also teaches that 'the love of money is the root of all evil…'

These two Bibles passages send us **important** warnings as to the impact of money in our lives, home and family. Jesus also focused our attention on the critical role money can play in our lives when He taught that 'you cannot serve two masters… you will love one and be disloyal (hate) the other…' Jesus at this point was literally comparing the pull God has on us as equal to the pull money can have on our heart. Jesus said, "You cannot serve God and Mammon (money) together.

The power that money wields over an individual if not controlled is immense and can be destructive, yet the solution and peace that money can bring is equally immense. So how do we deal with this dichotomy? Money is seriously needed in life and relationships; yet, money can destroy a family, home or relationship if not handled well.

The impact of the destructive nature of money can be summed up in these recent surveys:
A national survey by Money magazine reported, that

> **70 percent of married couples argue about money.**

It further wrote that most of the amounts spent were on frivolous purchases and this is high on the list of grievances.

Another survey carried out by Slater and Gordon summed up that,

> **Money worries are the leading cause of marriages falling apart.**

Lawyers have even through statistics, tagged the first working Monday of the year as "Divorce day" due to the number of requests for counselling. Most problems in homes, especially finance related problems, come to a head during the long holidays; in this case, the Christmas break.

The survey polled over 2,000 British adults and found that money worries top the list of reasons married couples split up; with 20% saying it was the biggest cause of marital strife.

Knowing this, the question becomes what practical steps can couples take to avoid becoming part of these negative statistics?

As a Chartered Accountant, Christian minister and counsellor, I have had many opportunities to listen to individuals and couples facing marital challenges, and I will be supporting the Slater and Gordon study through my observations and experiences with these individuals and couples, by saying that most marital challenges stem from monetary problems. Even when the problem presented is not initially financial, for example if the problem presented is about their child, most of the time, it somehow moves over to money.

A couple spoke to me about the challenge they were facing with their early teenage son, and I soon discovered that due to the need to 'keep financially afloat' (money) the couple took up extra jobs, and invariably, without being aware, neglected what was more important – the child. The lack of parental attention due to the quest to earn more (for whatever reason) soon began to reflect in the character, behaviour and academics of the child. Where care is not taken and corrective measures urgently put in place, we soon see a down-ward spiral of such children within the society. They fall prey to 'groomers' offering false family support and these youths are soon being used at the very least for petty crimes and in more serious cases, they are initiated into organised crime, gangs and gang violence. All because the cash strapped parents needed more money. I will speak more on children further down in the children's chapter.

Practical Ways of Managing Money Among Couples:

The first thing I say to couples is that it is possible to manage money on a physical day-to-day basis. It takes some basic financial skills to do this, and I always encourage people that all skills can be learnt if you are serious enough to want it. If a million pounds is at stake for you to learn and play a 5-minute piano piece in front of an audience at The Royal Albert Hall within a year, I can almost 100% guarantee that you will learn the piano to gain the prize. Everyone can learn any skill if their heart is set on it and they need it for survival. After all God said we should ask for wisdom if we lack it (James 1:5), and that we can do all things through Christ that strengthens us.

I encourage couples to acquire these basic financial skills by reading and attending short financial seminars and workshops. The myth surrounding financial jargons will be debunked and confidence and the desire to take control of your finances will increase astronomically. I should also mention here that financial skills are not only the premise of men as most people think. There are women who are also financially savvy. Whoever has the skills in a home should be given the purse to manage, but the other must also try and acquire basic skills and take an interest in managing the home's finances together.

Secondly, and on a spiritual but yet practical level, I encourage couples to be open and transparent in their financial dealings. They should see each other as ONE, playing for the same team. After all, the Bible tells us that both Adam and Eve stood naked (transparent) before each other, and were not ashamed (Gen. 2:25). This may be a challenging proposition in the 21st century, but it does not change or remove the biblical principle of transparency and honesty among couples.

One of the problems that spouses have shared with me about not being able to be transparent with their spouse is that they may end up being cheated or deprived of the money they worked for. I have also heard the excuse of lack of confidentiality – my spouse will know everything about me. In all these excuses, I simply see couples still lacking understanding of God's purpose for marriage; namely the two shall become one. This is why it is important for families to have prayer altars. If you are truly a believer, and you pray with your spouse and children daily, and you are still deceptive in your actions, (either through wanting to protect yourself from being cheated or cheating your spouse by taking advantage of his or her transparency through the fear of God and their trust in you), then you need to ask God to forgive you, and ask for grace and wisdom to implement God's purpose in your home.

Transparency, trust and honesty through active communication are key factors in aiding couples to successfully manage their finances. According to a recent survey by Ramsey Solutions, "Couples who say they have a "great" marriage are almost twice as likely to talk about money daily or weekly compared to those who say their marriage is "okay" or "in crisis."

Again, we see the need to talk about our finances. The more we talk, the more couples get closer and form tighter bonds in different aspects of their lives, including managing their finances. Expressing oneself in a relationship is also key to diffusing 'stored up' matters in the heart which eventually become explosive and unmanageable.

Below are four "Ds" to consider when managing family finance:

1   DELIBERATE TRUST:

Couples should start the godly management of their finances from a character of deliberate trust. Trust involves decision making. You must decide within yourself with God's grace to trust your spouse and also decide to act in such a way as to be trusted i.e. your actions should induce trust in your partner.

The principle of transparency, trust and openness which the bible encourages should be encouraged in a relationship. Once you begin to hide finances, you are already creating a crack in your marriage. Remember the enemy does not need a large door to enter your home and afflict you. All he needs is a crack.

A survey found that 25% of spouses are dishonest about their finances – in that they hide their spending habits from their spouse. Hiding expenditure from your spouse is almost an acceptance that you are misusing the funds God has given to the home and family. I have heard in many counselling sessions, the phrase, but I work for the money, it is my money and I can do whatever I like with it. As much as this is a fact, it is not the truth. I always say to spouses who say this that it would have been better if they were not married, because once you marry another person, you become one with them, and you should operate in trust and transparency with them irrespective of their actions. We are all accountable to God in the long run.

I also quickly remind them that it is God that gives the power to make wealth, and I am sure God's blessing is upon you partly because of your marriage relationship which in itself attracts God's favour. The Bible teaches that -

> "Also, we receive favour from men as we receive from God."

> "He that finds a wife, finds good thing and obtains favour before God."

Marriage induces God's favour upon a couple and invariably spills into people - employers, business partners, suppliers, customers, bank managers etc. favouring us even when they are not aware of this.

Selfishness, self-centeredness and excessive scrutiny can affect an individual from developing a mindset of trust and transparency in respect of family finance.

The danger of secret spending cost a couple I once counselled about thirty thousand pounds of savings. One was saving to buy their second flat, while the other through an uncontrollable spending habit and bad pyramid network investments, amassed huge debts on a credit card. Of course, this led to what uncontrollable debt always leads to - guilt, shame, fear of letting the other spouse know, stress, impatience and arguments. The arguments became terrible and just at the point it was getting to a head, the secret came out accidentally from a carelessly dropped bank letter. Put yourself in the betrayed spouse's shoes – picking up an innocent looking piece of paper only to see a bank letter with about thirty thousand pounds of debt staring at you. What would you do? How would you feel if that was you? That is what secret debt can do to a relationship. With counselling and renewed trust, the other spouse released their savings to pay the huge debts. The lesson I learnt from this couple is not only not to keep secret debts, but to quickly seek help before it becomes uncontrollable. 40% of the total debts were bank interests, penalties and charges. Consider your spouse in all of your actions. Your actions will have implications for both of you.

One of the best ways to avoid financial secrecy among couples is to give each other a monthly cash allowance that can be spent as they so wish without any question or discussion. This can be done by having a joint bank account for all household income and expenditure, but an individual account for each other's personal cash allowance.

I always encourage everyone to compensate themselves monthly for their hard work with at least 10% of their income. With couples, as they may earn different amounts, a percentage should be agreed by both as individual cash allowance. This will encourage trust, transparency and openness in the relationship while reducing or eliminating secrecy and unwarranted scrutiny.

2   DIFFERENCE:

I always tell couples to remember that they are different and were brought up by different parents, in dissimilar home, communities and sometimes cultures, thus compounding their differences.

I remember a story once told to me about a couple who nearly divorced because of toothpaste. The man was from a poor background and had learnt to appreciate, manage and save most things, while the wife was from a very rich background, and had never lacked for anything.

Their behaviours arising from their backgrounds soon became pronounced in the way they handled basic home supplies like toothpaste. The young man would press the toothpaste tube systematically from the bottom to the top to ensure the tube was totally empty. The young lady just pressed from anywhere as long as the toothpaste came out on her brush. This gradually degenerated into arguments as the man saw his wife as wasting the toothpaste while the lady saw her husband as wasting time and sweating the small stuff.

Some people love to save every little penny and enjoy living frugally to see their savings and investments grow or planning for years ahead, while others enjoy spending money at every reasonable opportunity, dealing with the immediate needs and living in the moment. To be honest, I have found out over years of counselling that neither is right nor wrong. That is why you need to understand the spending habits and style of your spouse before it becomes problematic in the home. Once you are aware of their spending habit, jointly seek a middle ground of compromise based on your financial objectives thus fostering peace in the home. Remember you are not right because you save or because you spend – the truth they say is always in the middle ground – that is the place of the cross, the place of grace.

To effectively manage money together despite your differences, take time to study and understand why your spouse spends or saves the way he or she does. What are they trying to achieve? Are they saving for your mutual future or the future of the children? Are they spending to fulfil joint obligations and responsibilities for yourselves and others? Does family background affect their spending style? What are their needs and wants? These are critical questions we must ask ourselves and seek to gain understanding of through communication and loving interactions before we start criticising the other. Once we gain better understanding of our spouse's spending habits and style, the couple should respect and celebrate these differences and use it to the advantage of their marriage union. Because spending styles and habits differ doesn't necessarily mean they are bad. A couple should identify their interests, strengths and opportunities that their spending style can fit into in the overall financial objectives of the family, and let them take charge of managing the finances in those areas.

Always seek to help your spouse create a conducive environment for active communication and seek a peaceful solution.

3 DESTINATION: Setting financial objectives and goals: Like any other project that has an objective to accomplish, couples should see their finances as a project with an end game. They should see it, for example, like sourcing for and travelling to a great holiday destination. The which, where, what, who, when and how of basic financial planning are questions that should be discussed and agreed upon to have the great holiday experience they both dream about.

Working together to get to your financial destination is important – leaving it to one person will mean that the other party may not enjoy the flight or the holiday destination chosen, but they have to make-do with it. That is the price of ignoring being involved in the planning and setting of financial goals together.

Financial goals can be set:
Weekly e.g. top up shopping, Monthly (e.g. from monthly shopping to paying bills), Yearly (e.g. cost of holiday) and Mid (3-5years planning - e.g. saving for deposit to buy a home); and Long term (5-10years and over e.g. pension and retirement plans, wills and other end-of-life plans).

Major financial goals may include the following:

- Annual holiday destination
- Renting or buying a home;
- Health and life insurance;
- Funding children's education
- Pension and other retirement plans
- Wider family support

I always encourage couples to set time apart, write their individual goals, and then reconcile this with their spouse and discuss and agree joint financial goals and how to fund each. This may feel like a chore for some, but you will soon get used to it, trust me. You may even start enjoying it. It brings couples closer anyway and that can only help the marriage union.

I used to be the person who prepared our financial papers and forwarded them to the tax office, but I gradually started encouraging my wife to learn how I was doing it. How relieved I was when she made her first submission to the tax office; and has been doing so for the past four years, although still with a little bit of support from me. She has gained a skill which cannot be taken away from her ever again. Encouraging your spouse to take interest in financial matters will invariably build trust and save more than time.

4 DISCUSS BUDGETS: Budget Together

Having good financial goals is just the first step, planning to achieve those goals becomes the next important thing. This is where budgeting comes in. Budgeting is simply a record of how much money is coming in – INCOME e.g. salaries, and what we are spending this money on – EXPENDITURE.

Both spouses should have a say in how much money is designated for which spending categories, e.g. savings, individual cash allowance, home running expenses, transport and travelling, children, retirement plan, etc. Deciding all these in advance by setting time aside in a good atmosphere of love and cooperation can only help reduce financial stress and increase trust and transparency.

Technology has made financial planning easier than before. There are many free user-friendly Apps on the market that can help in the family budgeting process.

One of the questions I get about budgeting is on income – how we should deal with our salaries. Should we have different bank accounts or a joint bank account? Of course, these questions come from couples who are both working to sustain the family. There are couples where only the husband or the wife works.

I always tell couples who both work that it all depends on the conditions of their hearts; how each spouse views money (is it master or servant?), and more importantly, the level of trust you have for your spouse.

Again, there is no right or wrong way. It all depends on understanding and trust.

The ideal, I always say, is to have a joint account where both spouses pay in their salaries and use it to pay all household and joint expenditures – from utilities to life insurance, by direct debit or standing orders. From this joint account, individual cash allowances can be transferred into individual personal bank accounts to be used as each spouse wishes. A joint email can be attached to the joint account where all emails and records from third parties are sent and kept for record purposes e.g. invoices, bills, receipts. This helps a couple put all their financial records in a central place and reduce papers.

Other ways include some couples having individual accounts, but sharing responsibilities, and each dealing with their areas of financial responsibility to the family.

There are other 'models' of banking that couples can adopt to manage their family finances, but whichever a couple chooses, they should always take professional advice especially on the implications of credit scores, tax matters and bank distress.

I personally encourage couples to have financial advisors, a coach or mentors especially for medium and long term plans.

8

CONFLICT RESOLUTION MANAGEMENT

Preferring One to Another

Conflict! This is one area most couples dread and would rather avoid talking about if given the opportunity. My wife and I were counselling a couple who were preparing to get married, and I remembered when we got to the conflict resolution session and introduced the topic as a discussion point for the session, the lady said, and I quote: "That is not our portion" – "God will not allow that to happen to us…" "I reject it in Jesus' name!"

As she uttered these statements in quick succession, I was taken aback and didn't know whether to laugh or cry for her naivety and her sincere desire to have a perfect relationship or to rebuke her for her ignorance. I could see how much she wanted their relationship not to have any conflict, and I wished I could make that happen or tell her what she would have loved to hear – that they would never come into any conflict throughout their married life. Oh, how I wished...But this is a ten session pre-marriage counselling course and only the truth will do.

My answer to this sweet lady was as I always start during this session:

– Conflict is a matter of 'WHEN' in marriage or any relationship and not 'IF'

The key is how you prepare and handle conflict when it rears its ugly head.

Conflict started when the devil was able to have a discussion with Eve in the Garden of Eden, and by the end of their meeting, humanity had failed God. God being a fair and just God had to apply the needed punishment by placing curses on Adam, Eve and the serpent. I will encourage you to do a thorough study of Genesis 3 especially with regard to the curses God pronounced on these three, and you will understand more about conflict in the home.

In the parable of the wise and foolish builder (Matthew 7:24-27 NIV) bold emphasis on mine:

> [24] *"Therefore everyone who hears these words of **mine** and puts them into practice is like a wise man who built his house on the rock. [25] The rain came down, the streams rose, and the winds blew and beat against that house; yet it did not fall, because it had its foundation on the rock. [26] But everyone who hears these words of mine and does not put them into practice is like a foolish man who built his house on sand. [27] The rain came down, the*

streams rose, and the winds blew and beat against that house, and it fell with a great crash."

Jesus taught that "the rain came..." in some versions, the rain is termed the storm. Storms will come to the wise builder and also to the foolish builder. It's only a matter of time. Surviving the period of the storm will depend on how much you have prepared for the storm. What sort of materials have you been using to build your home? The storm is coming, and it will expose all shoddy craftsmanship in any relationship.

No season of life is permanent. In the west, there are four main seasons – Summer, Autumn, Winter and Spring; and none is permanent. Marriages also go through different seasons – some seasons lasting longer than others. What you do in the different seasons will contribute to the overall survival of your marriage.

If like me, you watch nature programmes, then you must have noticed how some animals prepare for different seasons – especially the winter seasons. They work hard in the summer and autumn storing food for the winter season, as the harsh winter weather will affect food supply. So I encourage couples that as they enjoy the summer seasons of their marriage, they should spare a thought and prepare for those winter seasons ahead as well. The periods when even hibernation may be necessary for eventual survival of the home and family.

Now that we know it's a matter of time before conflict happens in a relationship, it will be good to explore attitudes that will aid in early diffusion of these conflicts when they come.

The following are some of such positive attitudes:

1 *Determine to resolve conflicts quickly– Time is of the essence*

In conflict, the first and most important task for each spouse is to determine within themselves to seek resolution of the conflict in peace as soon as possible. This is a decision and rule that couples should seek to live by. We are going to offend each other at some point, so why not agree during the 'time of peace' on how to resolve conflict when it shows up.

I feel this is why Paul wrote in Ephesians 4:26-27 (emphasis mine):

"In your **anger** do not **sin**: Do not let **the sun go down** while you are still angry, and do not give the **devil a foothold**."

From the above scripture, we can see that in conflict, there is hurt and anger, but Paul is admonishing us not to let this result in SIN (rage, violence, unforgiveness, murder etc.) and he was giving us the antidote for avoiding the anger and hurt leading to sin – QUICK RESOLUTION. We must remember as the bible teaches, that "We wrestle not against flesh and blood but against principalities and powers…"Ephesians 6:10-12. The source of the conflict is not your spouse, but the enemy of your soul. He has just used your spouse's weakness or lapses to get to you.

When you allow incidents in the home to fester, it will one day lead to sin, so do not let the sun go down on your anger. Not heeding to this instruction of quick resolution will invariably "give the devil a foothold" in your heart and your home. You have officially but unknowingly opened the door of your heart to the enemy, and you are having discussions with the enemy about what your spouse has done and what you should now do about it. You will not get a brownie point for guessing the type of advice the enemy will suggest to you. It will definitely not be godly advice. It may sound like it, but look into it properly, and you will see that it will lead to the destruction of the home you are building for God. In fact you will probably feel good about the advice, but they're suggestions that will only satisfy your own ego and craving for revenge and nothing more. You have started to build on the sand instead of building on the rock.

Not seeking quick and whole-hearted resolution of a conflict sets us against God. In The Lord's Prayer, (Matthew 6:15), we read "… forgive us our sins as we forgive those who sin against us…" – this is a conditional statement that clearly shows that God forgiving us is directly linked to us forgiving others. Mulling over what our spouse has done to us, and throwing 'pity parties' by reporting to everyone except your spouse, will just complicate your life further. Stop holding grudges, stop the 'cold-shoulder' treatment, stop ignoring your spouse, attempt to get the matter resolved, help to make it easy to 'kill-off' the conflict.

We all offend God daily and we seek His forgiveness daily; imagine God ignoring you at the time you need Him most because you don't deserve His forgiveness as you have not forgiven others. If this is not a position you wish to find yourself in, especially at Christ's coming, always seek to resolve and forgive your spouse and others at the earliest opportunity.

The parable of the unforgiving servant (Matthew 18:30-35) teaches us lessons. We owe God a lot and He forgives us daily but then we want our own debtors (those who have offended us) to pay fully what they owe us. We become the Merchant of Venice who in wanting a pound of flesh lost everything! Unforgiveness is a spirit of wickedness that prefers to see others suffer.

Prolonged conflicts characterised by unforgiveness, has turned most homes into the devil's playground with lying, bitterness, envy, jealousy, insecurity, conniving, manipulation, control and many more ills now the order of the day.

I once heard a story of a man who didn't treat a cut on his leg and eventually lost the leg through amputation. This is sometimes the story of many homes – they ignore the painful process of treatment only to lose a vital part of their existence.

A marriage where spouses hold grudges, bitterness and anger towards one another is a marriage devoid of prayer and most likely of the presence of God. Where the 'family altar' is not serviced, and the fire goes out upon the altar, occasion has been given to the enemy to attack and bring destruction to the home. Children, finances and health are mostly the casualties of this ungodly act.

I have heard in many counselling sessions that one of the spouses is always being stubborn – my encouragement to the other is to keep being the available one for God to use to bring about His purpose. We know we can't force the other spouse to forgive us or make peace, but it should not be for lack of trying. We must keep the bond of peace as grace is granted to us; we must continually seek to resolve issues early. Romans 12:18 summed this up beautifully -"If it is possible, as far as it depends on you, live at peace with everyone."

Are you living in peace with your spouse? or are you living in unforgiveness, grudges and anger? It's time to turn your sword into a ploughing instrument and seek peace through God's grace and wisdom. It's time to ask for

God's wisdom (James 1:8) and bring back God's peace into your marriage and home. Do not let your home be a casualty.

2 Patience and Perseverance – Winning qualities

Conflict in a relationship does not just happen once; in fact, issues can surface again and again, but does this then mean that the relationship is doomed? NO… the enemy may want you to think like that and start your 'bail-out' process, but I tell you, each conflict a couple overcomes can only make them stronger as they learn and progress in their married life; the active words here being 'Learn and Progress' since constant bickering and arguments without learning and improving from them can be fatally damaging to the relationship.

We must understand as I earlier mentioned, that couples are from different homes, families, communities and sometimes countries, and so, they will have different values. All these can affect relationships and bring about conflicts. But as said previously, the key is gaining an understanding of this, and being determined to work these differences out amicably with God's wisdom and maturity.

In exploring the Bible on dealing with conflict, we soon find out that God allows this for a reason. There is a purpose in the mind of God to use conflict in relationships – Romans 8:28 says, *"All things work together for good for them that love God and are the called according to His purpose."* ALL THINGS – including all our relational conflicts; God will cause them to give us an expected end of God's goodness.

In Romans 5:3-4, we see Paul the Apostle telling us that trials produce perseverance and perseverance produces character and character, hope. This is amazing! Is Apostle Paul telling us we stand to gain the ability to withstand challenging times (perseverance), and that this ability to stand challenging situations will then invariably lead us to the 'High Street' of God's character? The same character expressed in Galatians 5:22- called the 'fruit of the spirit' – love, joy, gentleness etc. thus making us to live like Christ? Yes.

So perseverance produces this character in us – not just fasting and praying which also helps, but hope is produced through character formation not 'wishful thinking' type of hope but the very Hope that makes not ashamed (Romans 5:5-11); the hope that actually produces and delivers its objectives. The hope of Eternal life in Christ, the joy of a happy, godly home, your 'great expectation' nursed for your marriage and home; all stemming from managing our relational conflicts well. No wonder James admonished us in James 1:3-4 to allow perseverance to do its full job: *"Let perseverance finish its work so that we can become mature and complete, not lacking anything."* By the time we allow perseverance to complete its assignment in us, we would have become MATURE, no longer acting, behaving or exhibiting childish tendencies like petulance, manipulations, control and tantrums. They all cease, because you are now mature, hoping and trusting your deliverance to Christ. This is the state of completion where you do not worry for or lack anything. You are not driven by anything or anyone but you are rested in Christ's peace in all things. What a state to be in.

This of course contradicts the world's way of handling conflict. The world advocates defending your position strongly, retaliating robustly, and if you are tired of it all, quitting and getting another life. The world uses clichés like: life is too short to be enduring this pain, seek alternatives, I am not a foot mat, or you only have one life.

No wonder the divorce rate is 51% – which has increased drastically from the sixties. We are now in a world of the fast life and most people expect their marriage to deliver on their expectations fast and if it doesn't meet their expectations, they quit. "Bearing with each other" is now an ancient philosophy, but it will benefit us as a society if we bring such concepts back.

Perseverance is a word that depicts bearing up under a load. I liken this to a weight lifting contest. In the 'clean and jerk,' you are expected to lift the heavy weight above your head and hold it for a few seconds (which feels like a life time of torture) until you get green lights from at least two of the three judges grading you. If not, you may have to come back again. It takes just about five seconds of staying stable under the weight and that's it, you've done it.

Relationship conflicts can be likened to that. There are times in the relationship that we are tested like a weightlifter expected to bear a weight. These are heavy weights that no one would want to bear, but really they only last a few seconds and heaven gives us the thumbs up to go to the next category – we are promoted to the next class weight, we are rewarded for making the grades in that category and our ranking 'climbs' higher, we have mastered that weight, we have matured in that category.

Ask any weightlifter about this, and most will tell you that during the weight bearing, they really wanted to quit, but the next class, or the gold, silver or bronze is enough motivation to just stay that few seconds longer.

So if you are thinking of quitting, consider the price of pleasing Christ, of making your home a godly example in an evil world; consider the many that are soldiering on just because they see you ahead. They may not even know the weight you are under, but you have inspired them to keep going. Now consider the implications on these if you quit now. Consider your testimony in Christ, and consider the negative impact of a broken home on your children, your spouse and the society. Yes, the weight is heavy, yes the weight is unbearable, but tap into the grace of God to keep going and let perseverance complete its work in you! Don't quit; persevere. Pray for grace to persevere.

I always encourage couples to go back to the

vow they made in the presence of God and many witnesses when they were getting married. I have noticed over the years of counselling couples that most couples seem not to remember their vows – the excitement of the wedding day robs them of the importance of their vows. They spend most of the time focused on getting the colours, the train, the gowns, the cake, etc. They miss the most important thing in the marriage process – their vows made before God and witnesses to each other. In the last quarter of this year, I have had the opportunity and grace to marry two couples – and I ensured during their ten sessions of counselling, they read and understood their vows before going through with them. I even gave them a chance to reconsider their position after we had gone through the vows, as I believe a broken engagement is far better than a broken marriage. Marriage, I always tell couples, is hard work. It should be fully prepared for, with this in mind marriage is not a walk in the park but requires dedication and focus.

3 Determine to build not destroy – a choice to be made

We have spoken extensively about the need to be patient with each other and to bear each other's burdens through perseverance, but another grace we should seek in dealing with conflicts is to be determined to be a builder of your home and not a destroyer.

Some may be "patient" and be "persevering," but with the mindset of plotting and planning a way out. So we should never assume that because someone is quiet, they are truly persevering or being patient with the situation – there may be anger, bitterness or unforgiveness in their hearts.

The determination and choice to build a home in the fear and love of God must be taken by the individual spouse. This choice and determination will help spouses to take 'builders' decisions in the face of crises and conflicts. Such partners have made up their mind not to quit, they have made up their mind to go the long-haul. I saw a caption on a friend's display picture of their Whatsapp account, and it read:

> "YOU JUST CAN'T BEAT THE PERSON WHO NEVER GIVES UP"

This sentence characterises a spouse that has made up their mind with the help of God to build for God and not to quit.
They see their marriage as God giving them a piece of land away from their parents to build another home and make it habitable, beautiful and filled with God's presence. This is a project that will take time, effort, determination, focus and many more graces. From clearing the land, to breaking the ground and building the foundation, to putting the pillars and structures in place, to roofing it, painting it and equipping it with modern conveniences to make it habitable for God's presence and your children and anyone that visits you.

The question is what will you contribute to the building of this home in word and in action? As a builder, would you say you are contributing positively to the building project? Or are you undermining the effort of your spouse? Do you find your own joy in being a disruptive builder? Or are you one that maximises the time? Do you sit back and honestly assess your contribution and efforts in your marriage? Looking through all the "Cs" we have been exploring, can you honestly say you are making good and godly efforts in building your home, or are you always opening your home to internal and external threats that set your building project back consciously or unconsciously? Everyone must honestly and heartily consider this and where necessary, repent and change their ways; and if you have been truly an honest and hardworking builder, it's time to increase the pace and maximise grace.

Build with good words, build with forgiveness, build with mercy, build with love, build with submission to each other, build with fostering peace, build with action, build with prayer and see your home thrive as a reward of your choice and sacrifice to build for God. Remember, marriage is not primarily about us, but about God using marriage to showcase the relationship of Christ with His body. Keep sowing a good seed to get a great harvest (Galatians 6:7). Uproot and take life away from evil seeds sown through harsh words and actions. Uproot the seed of criticism and contention. Commend and compliment instead. Uproot the seed of ignoring and neglecting your spouse, and plant the seed of increased intimacy and interest. Remember whatever we sow, we shall reap. Expect a great harvest of God's goodness as we review our self in the microscope of God's word. Repent and redeem lost grounds.

4 Develop a godly character – cultivate and produce good fruit

The bible teaches that by their fruits we shall

know them.

We have also heard that 'charity begins at home'. The family home is the place that tests what nature or manner of individual you are or what spiritual stuff you are made of.

If you have a friend or colleague that always gets you on the wrong side, you can devise a means of ignoring them – block their number, stop relating with them actively. Avoid them as much as possible, or apply other legal means as may be necessary to distance yourself from them. With your spouse, this is near impossible. You wake up on the same bed, you probably use the same bathroom, eat together, go to family functions together, attend children's school meetings together, so ignoring or avoiding them is not possible. This is where the cultivation and application of the 'fruit of the Spirit' becomes necessary.

Not only should you cultivate and regularly apply the 'fruit of the spirit', but you must also daily mortify the 'deeds of the flesh.' These are like dangerous weeds that have always occupied the land but which had to be cleared to make room for good fruits.

A quick reminder of what the Bible teaches us in Galatians 5: 16-26 about the works of the flesh and the fruit of the Spirit is necessary.

Daily we must consciously apply the 'fruit of the Spirit' in our relationship with our spouse and others, and likewise, we must daily also mortify the works of the flesh. The fruit of the Spirit is about growing in the character of God, while growth in the works of the flesh is about growing in the character of the devil and the world. We are in the world, but our character is not of the world.

I recently bought a farm land, and it was shocking to see how much was spent in clearing and treating the land, in order to get it ready for the planting season. I liken this to the price paid to buy and clear our sin ravaged hearts from Satan by God through Christ Jesus.

The wild weeds of sin had ravaged our hearts, reigned unchecked for years as wild weeds takeover farm land – growing and expanding their territories daily, until the land was bought by another person. We have been bought with a price – the blood of Jesus Christ through his death, and so we, like that land, now belong to God and God has decided to clear and clean up our hearts by the blood of Christ and has planted the seed of His Spirit in our hearts to grow in grace and produce wholesome character and harvest. May we be productive in our Christian walk and works.

I should add here that the clearing of the weeds is a daily/weekly process in the farm, as the weeds always find a way of growing back. In the same way, our hearts must daily be checked to ensure that any wild weed of sin is mortified – uprooted and killed off, while ensuring the fruits are watched over jealously, tended, watered, pruned and kept safe till they are harvested. What great joy comes to the farmer's heart during a good harvest! May

God be joyful over your marriage and your home in Jesus' name, amen.

5 Don't underestimate the power of communication – Have a discussion

In conflict resolution, communication is always at the centre of solutions. Many problems can easily be overcome by having a healthy discussion on the matter. Of course, this may involve sacrifices, compromises and

conceding some ground in negotiations, but moving forward should definitely include early discussions. The earlier we come to the 'round table' of discussion, the better for the survival and effectiveness of our relationship. In Isaiah 1, God said come let us reason together. God has shown here the power of communication in conflict resolution. If God can call us to a discussion to sort out our problems with Him, how much more us with one another.

Communication and discussion should be the hallmark of a good relationship.

We recently heard the agreement entered into by USA with North Korea on denuclearisation. This only happened after intense discussions and concessions. Similarly with the global warming agreement of nations. It took about 98% of nations coming together, discussing, negotiating and conceding grounds, to be able to reach this important agreement to save the planet from global warming. Why am I going into all of this? Just to drive it home that no civil relationship, talk less of a spiritual one can move forward in a conflict situation without communication and discussions. I will refer you to the earlier point on communication, and hence will not spend too much time on this.

Someone who comes to the roundtable for discussion must come with an open mind, not with preconceived notions or selfishness. They must genuinely want and seek a solution, must value the relationship, and must be willing to sacrifice and if necessary, concede some grounds. Such an individual must see the relationship as vital to their own existence and to their moving forward.

6 Selflessness and sacrifice – a price worth paying

It took God the sacrifice and the shedding of the blood of His son Jesus Christ on the cross of Calvary to reconcile us back to himself. What a price to pay to restore a relationship. John 3:16 says, for God so loved the world that he gave His only begotten son. Love propelled God to sacrifice Christ.

You can't sacrifice without the character and the spirit of love operating within you. Love compelled God, and it is love that should and would compel us to sacrifice. I am not surprised, then, when I go through the various marriage vows.

Love always seems to be at the centre of it all. We must love truly, dearly and wholeheartedly for there to be any grace to give and sacrifice. I remember when my fiancée and I(now my wife) were still courting, with the marriage date set, only to be told she had six months to live because her blood cells were attacking each other and the projection was a maximum of six months. This came as a shock to everyone, and this was the same lady the Lord told me was my wife. I couldn't accept this, and God gave me grace to wait upon Him for forty days – that was the first time in my life of waiting upon God that long. The situation demanded drastic measures and sacrifices, and I received grace for this. A week after the fasting and waiting, she had a hospital appointment and that was where she was told that the problem reversed itself inexplicably. Praise God! And of course our wedding plans moved on a gear quicker. I had two options when the news came, call off all plans and start seeking another future partner, or be selfless and allow the spirit of love to compel me to pay the price of waiting on God. Thank God I took the latter route which became part of our testimonies and victories in Christ. It is important to really hold our relationship dear in our hearts and always seek opportunities to sacrifice to make it better and fruitful.

The opposite of selflessness is selfishness – a condition where all you think and do is for yourself and yourself only. You are only consumed with increasing and bettering yourself even if it involves destroying or cheating others. Pleasing oneself becomes all consuming. A selfish person cannot sacrifice and if they do, their sacrifice is shoddy. They feel the cost and react unpleasantly about it everytime. Abel gave his sacrifice out of a heart of love for God and his sacrifice was accepted, while Cain gave a selfish sacrifice. No thought went into it. Many a time, we behave like Cain in our marriage relationship and become selfish and self-consumed in the way we relate to our spouse especially in handling conflicts. Let us seek that all we do in our homes and marriages to take them forward, comes from a heart of love, selflessness and great sacrifice; so that God may accept our sacrifice as He accepted the sacrifice of Abel.

7 Avoid Pride – Seek help early

There are times in a marriage that having a round table discussion with each other does not bring progress. This is not because discussions and communicating with each other doesn't work, but one or both parties have come to the table with their own preconceived decision and is unwilling to concede any ground. In such instances, rather than just packing it all up or allowing the problem to fester, as a result of pride, we must humble ourselves and seek third party help early. The bible teaches that 'in the multitude of counsel there is safety'.

I know most couples find it difficult to seek third party help, but I always encourage couples even before conflict arises to agree between themselves which one or two elders they can both go to for solving difficult issues. Both couples must respect and honour this elder/counsellor and the elder/counsellor must be God-fearing, seek the success of the couple's marriage, be Holy Spirit filled, have a successful standing marriage and be very experienced in godly marriage counselling.

Going to a marriage advisor is not a mark of failure but rather signifies a determination to make a success of your home and marriage.

Over the years, I have observed that it's the men that are mostly reluctant to go for counselling, and I personally put this down to ego and pride. They don't want to sit in front of another man or woman and recount incidents and issues. It doesn't sit well with most men, but the bible encourages counselling. Some women can also take this stand mostly because they do not see a need for it or they don't feel that any notable change will come out of it. To this group, I will encourage you to do the best in your power to seek counsel since giving up is not a godly option. The enemy behind your conflict is waiting for your marriage to fail so he can claim another victory. You can't afford for the enemy of your soul and your home to take glory over your home.

Getting to the point of suggesting or inviting an elder/counsellor simply means one party was not ready to talk or give concessions, and to save the marriage, an elder/counsellor had to be invited to arbitrate between the couple.

After all, in Matthew 18:16-17 the bible states: 'But if he will not listen, take one or two others along, so that 'every matter may be established by the testimony of two or three witnesses.' If he refuses to listen to them, tell it to the church; and if he refuses to listen even to the church, treat him as you would a pagan or a tax collector. My two examples above tell me that a chance has been given to the offending person who in the case of conflict, might even be the person that is claiming to have suffered the hurt; the point being that the individual has refused to listen to the other, and by so doing, has made resolution impossible. This creates the need to take one or two others along, (elders/counsellors), for breakthrough and moving forward.

Forgiveness is also a key element in conflict resolution. We must be willing to forgive. It is not easy, but we must have it in our hearts to want to forgive, and allow the Holy Spirit to do his work in us and through us. After all, we all offend God, and we seek and receive

His forgiveness. Likewise, we should also seek to forgive others who have wronged us. The disciple of Christ asked him, how many times should I forgive my brother? Jesus' answer, I am sure shocked those present, and is still shocking everyone today. You must accommodate seventy times seven wrongs in a day, before you have any right not to forgive! 490 times a day. Jesus is just telling us to forgive no matter what, as 490 offenses in a day by one person is near impossible.

In conclusion, conflict in marriage must always be recognised as an attack on your home. Just as it was in the Garden of Eden when the serpent deceived Eve and made her eat the fruit of the knowledge of good and evil, and she in turn offered it to Adam, the devil is still prowling around looking for casualties of his deception. The consequence of falling is a loss of peace, tranquillity and harmony. Maintain the peace of God in your home, deal with conflicts early, and invite a counsellor where necessary.

9
COMMUNITIES

Families, Friends et al

The bible teaches in Genesis 2:24-25: "Therefore shall a man *leave his father and his mother* and shall *cleave unto his wife*: and they shall be *one flesh*. 2:25 And they were *both naked*, the man and his wife, and *were not ashamed*."

These verses tell us that the key people in a marriage union are: the man (husband) and the woman (wife). This is an area that some spouses find difficult to understand. From God's perspective, a man must leave (but not abandon) his parents, and start a new family for God by cleaving (a joining of heart, mind and purpose) to his wife, and they both grow until they are one in every area of oneness; where transparency (nakedness) and acceptance (no shame) becomes a vital component and bedrock of their relationship.

With this in mind, does that mean that married couples must ostracise everyone in their lives? The obvious answer is no! We cannot build our family in isolation of others; because we are not an island. We are surrounded by people, and visions can't be accomplished without God putting others in line to aid the success of that vision, and marriage is not exempted from this. There is no marriage that can successfully accomplish its objective or survive without the input of extended family, friends and other people with whom God has surrounded the marriage. Some cultures even see the marriage of two people as a marriage of two families rather than of just a couple. The key is knowing who God has sent and for what reason at every point of the marriage. As it is popularly said, some friends are for a reason, some for a season, and some for life. Discernment by the Spirit of God should help us know who is who and when and how each individual should be present in our lives. We must consciously want to seek God's leading in handling everyone around us. It is advisable to live a life of constantly committing our ways before God, and He will always direct our paths, even in our relationships.

We know that there are some people that may wield indirect or direct influence on our marriage union rightly or wrongly. Knowing this to be the case, this chapter deals with how couples in a marriage relationship ought to relate with this group of people. Do they really have the right to wield such potent influence on our marriages?

The bible teaches that, 'we shall know the truth, and the truth shall set us free...' - The best way to know what to do with anyone in any of these groups in our lives is to explore the truth of God's word, and in obedience, implement it without fear or favour through the power of the Holy Spirit.

Once you find and walk in the light of God's truth, through His Spirit, you will not stumble or grope about in the darkness of people's fears, manipulations, connivance or control. The truth you know and walk in will set you free of any fear, guilt or doubt. You will become bold and strong and with God's strength, start removing ungodly influences of negative powers and emotions over your life, your spouse, your children, your marriage and your home.

We must at the very least know what the bible teaches on the following two key groups which I have termed;

- The unlisted guests – good to have, but not required;
- The listed guests – those who the bible say are important to our marriage union;
  - Why the bible says they are important and;
  - How the bible requires us to deal with them.

The Unlisted Guests – *Good to have but not required:*

Many times, we include people who do not have any business influencing our marriage in the limited list God allows, and they in turn, through our ignorance, foolishness or fear influence us to the point of making our marriage ineffective or worse still, aid us in the destruction of our marriage and home. The key word here is 'influence.' We may have friends and family surrounding us, but are they having undue influence; affecting the dynamics of our home? This is the question we must answer.

This list may include friends, (church friends, school

mates, colleagues, social mates etc.) and family (including siblings, cousins, aunties, uncles, and the list goes on). I have many counselling stories that I can share to support this claim that some people wield influence on our marriage and home to the point of controlling one spouse or both, and invariably damage their marriage union, sometimes, irrevocably.

We must understand that most 'hangers on' are there for their own selfish ends. They need you to continue to be what you used to be to them, to be there for them as you used to be before you got married, and once this changes, some may embark (knowingly or unknowingly)

directly or indirectly on a campaign to get you back. They can use all sorts of satanic tools available to them, from lying to manipulation to connivance to control, and before you realise it, you have begun to have conflict in your home. When that happens, who do you turn to? You still turn to "them;" and their satanic advice continues, at which point your heart becomes troubled and confused, trust is lost in the home, suspicion becomes pronounced, and selfishness instead of selflessness and sacrifice takes over. All because you undiscerningly and foolishly allowed interference, or brought in someone that God has not asked you to bring into your home to influence and control you.

We need to understand that it is not every member of our family (even siblings) or friends that wish us well; this may not sound nice, but it is the truth. Some envy you, some are jealous about your progress, and some just want to compete with you, of which you may not even be aware. They want the type of house you have, the type of car you drive, the type of spouse you have, the type of salary or job you have, and the list goes on!

Look at that quote again:-"Some friends are for a

reason, some for a season and some for life". When we hang unto people - (family, friends or colleagues) who God has sent to our lives for a reason or a season, and they have accomplished their purpose in our life, but we still for reasons best known to us stubbornly hold on to them tight, they will soon become a tool in the hand of the enemy against us and against our home, and it's our fault. Be spiritually sensitive. Scan those around you prayerfully, and follow the instruction of the Holy Spirit in dealing with them.

You may be feeling the need to hang on to these people because you see and use them probably as a sounding board for what is going on in your life or home or as comforters to soothe the pains of challenges at home (a crutch to lean on). Instead of that, why not seek to learn more about your spouse and tell them those challenges you feel you are facing in your home. I will always encourage couples to invest more in their home and marriage rather than taking this 'investment' of time, and communication outside the home.

At the end of the day, God is only going to ask you about the assignment and the purpose He has given you to accomplish, of which your spouse is an integral part of, not about outsiders.

Imagine if you are being tested in an Economics exam, but have spent most of your time reading Biology for leisure during an exam period. Will it surprise you if you fail the main exam of Economics? That's what most people do – investing their time and effort in a company they do not have shares in – no long term benefit, other than liking their product. That's wrong. Invest more time and energy on your spouse. Drastically reverse the trend and reduce the time and effort you invest in unprofitable friends and family. Rather, invest it in your spouse and home and see what God will do.

Please don't misunderstand me here. I am not saying you should let go of your family and friends, as sometimes God uses them for us. What I am saying is don't give them that place of influence in your home which God has not given them. Don't let them control your life at the detriment of the assignment God has given you to build your home.

Of course, I still have my siblings, families and friends

around me. I have my brothers and sisters in law, and we get on very well; but there are discussions I will not have with them, and there are influences I will not let them have on me to the point of adversely affecting my home. A friend once called me a fool for trying to pay off our home's mortgage early. When I asked why, he said, your wife can start trouble and take the house from you. When I told him that my wife is a signatory to all my accounts, he was baffled, and said that I was really being stupid. I told him that all I do in life is to please God, and ensure my wife is secure; and if my wife decides to take the house, well, it has always been for her and the children anyway, but God who knows everything and pays everyone their due reward will see both hearts and judge accordingly.

This is a good friend, and he was concerned for me, but his concerns were drawn from the world's pool of fleshly advice and not from God's Word nor His heart of love, sacrifice and selflessness, so I rejected that advice. This is a choice we all have to make when advice comes to us from those who actually want our good. We need to line their advice up with God's Word, and make an informed decision. Take or leave the counsel, ensuring you are not lending yourself to undue influence or control.

On another instance, one other friend became furious because she thought my wife was neglecting me. I didn't know she was monitoring everything. She would call early in the morning, and after pleasantries, she would ask after my wife, and innocently, I would say she had left for work. This friend would call in the evening and go through the same motions, and most times my wife would not be back from work and I would say so innocently. On this fateful day she became very angry with me and my wife and said it was wicked of my wife to keep leaving home early and coming back late, and that she must be taking me for a fool. I tried explaining to her that my wife works in the school system as an assistant principal, and she has to be in school before the students start coming in, as well as attend late meetings after school. All my explanations fell on deaf ears. She went on with the mindset that I was always making excuses for my wife. Well, that day opened my eyes to how people can monitor you without your knowing. She is a good friend of the family, and probably cares for our wellbeing, but I had to draw a line, as her advice and suggestions, noble as they may have been, were not going to help my home. These are decisions you must take, to scan people that surround you and put them where God wants you to put them – mostly at arm's length!

What am I saying? I am not saying you should become a hermit and not have friends or family around, but put them where God puts them. When a friend or family member starts to advise you, and you see a detrimental impact in your home, it's time to call a time out with that friend or family.

Sentiments and tradition sometimes make it difficult for some people to draw that line, but it is a line that you must have to draw for the sake of what is important to you – your spouse, your children and your home. Any action outside this may be highlighting selfishness in you as a person, as you prefer the cosy comfort of people like that rather than focusing on your God given assignment.

The Listed Guests – *Invited and honoured:*

In fact, no one is on this list, as God expects the man and the woman to work with Him and His Spirit in covenant to build their home and fulfil the purpose for which He has brought them together. The only person allowed to stir and influence you as husband or wife must be the Holy Spirit. This should not take away the fact that God sometimes sends people to us to help us in the achievement of our purpose. The people God sends to you should be helpers and not detractors or distractions to your God given assignment of building your home. They must be helpers in getting you to your destiny. Looking at Ephesians 6:1-4, we see two key groups of people – 'Parents in the Lord' and 'Biological or Adopted Parents'. These are people the couple are meant to obey, respect and honour - a very limited list of people that may influence you through their prayer and counsel.

Let us explore this group further through Ephesians 6:1-4:

> $^{6:1}$ *Children, obey your parents in the Lord: for this is right.*
> $^{6:2}$ *Honour thy father and mother; which is*

the first commandment with promise;
6:3 That it may be well with thee, and thou mayest live long on the earth.
6:4 And, ye fathers, provoke not your children to wrath: but bring them up in the nurture and admonition of the Lord.

Parents in the Lord:

Couples should have people in their lives that they respect and honour and are willing to submit to in counsel. Challenges will come, storms will rage, and these are times you may need the input of your spiritual parents. The bible teaches that in the multitude of counsel there is safety. There is a safety spiritual parents bring from their godly guidance and counsel. God still uses people to get us to our destiny, and spiritual parents are some of such people. I always encourage couples to see their spiritual parents in this capacity – advisor, counsellor, mentor and coach. Spouses must not let pride tell them they have no need of spiritual parents. A look into Moses' life will tell us that if it was not for the advice of his father-in-law, Jethro, he would have burnt himself out in ministry and may never have accomplished what God did through him for the children of Israel. Newly married couples have never 'walked this path' before, and will do well to seek advice and guidance from spiritual parents during times they are needed.

Spiritual parents are not there to compete with you, but to ensure that you run the race of life with diligence and ensure your life gives glory to God through Christ Jesus.

An African adage says; "No matter how bad a child becomes, the parents cannot give the child to the lion to devour." This is where I see the role of spiritual parents clearly. They are able to help you to stand up, clean up and aid you in moving forward to achieving your purpose. Spiritual parents must be ready and willing to challenge and rebuke ungodly actions without fear or favour.

A spiritual parent must want the good of the couple, and their 'pride' is seeing the couple flourish and prosper in life and ministry. Spiritual parents must not abuse their exalted position by manipulating or controlling the couple for their own benefit or gain. Couples should prayerfully consider those who should fill this role.

Once a couple has sought counsel from their spiritual parents, they should obey. The bible says this is right before God. Couples must not fall into the danger of disobeying counsel, because it didn't meet their expectations. This in itself is dangerous. Couples should avoid this by giving full information on all matters before a decision is taken. They should be truthful, plain and honest when seeking advice. No one goes to the doctor and keeps part of the information of their symptoms to themselves because maybe they are ashamed. You will get the wrong diagnosis and you will be endangering your health.

Couples should therefore, ensure full disclosure when seeking counsel – explore options with their spiritual parents, and whatever advice is given, should be considered seriously and followed.

In summary:

Spiritual parents should:

- Know the couple they are mentoring, which comes from forming a relationship with them through spending time with them in prayers and encouragement;

- Know and appreciate the calling and gifting of God upon the couples' lives as individuals and as couples. Prayerfully gaining understanding of God's assignment and the seasons they are in.

- Spiritual parents should be willing to make spiritual sacrifices in fasting and praying for the couple, releasing where possible, financial and other resources to helping the couple fulfil their godly purpose;

- With godly wisdom and humility, rebuke where necessary; without fear or favour, bringing correction and spiritual encouragement in the process;

- Consistently seek to mentor, train and establish couples in their God-given purpose.

- Teach them to understand the voice of God – helping them to be spiritually independent in their decision making. Eli taught Samuel to hear and answer to the voice of God.

- Spiritual parents must not be controlling in anyway – their job is to give counsel and let the couples take their decision and work with them through the decision taken.

Spiritual Children (The Couple) should:

- Seek God in prayer before choosing spiritual parents: Couples should remember that the Bible teaches that 'children should obey their spiritual parents' and with this in mind, couples should understand that they will at one point in their married life, follow the advice of a spiritual parent which may have consequences. They should thus ensure they take this task of choosing a spiritual parent seriously as it may influence decisions and actions taken in the family.

- Build a relationship with your spiritual parents: Most people are busy in their lives, including your chosen spiritual parents, so it is your responsibility as a couple to form a good relationship with your spiritual parents. Call, text, set visiting appointments, serve and help where possible. These all contribute to you forming a strong relationship and spiritual bond with them. An African adage says; "It' is a child that stretches forth its hands that will first be carried by an elder." You have to show your spiritual parents that you desire, value and honour their presence and contributions in your life. You must not let them feel that it's a forced relationship. You only get a double portion of their grace if you stick close as Elisha did to Elijah;

- Trust is a big issue in any relationship. You must build trust with your spiritual parents with prayers, and of course, based on their advice antecedents;

- Be a blessing to your spiritual parents. I encourage couples to give to spiritual parents. They probably will not need your present or financial gifts, but it shows your heart, and stirs theirs to always bless and continually keep you in their prayers.

Biological or Adopting Parents:
(Father & Mother)

Although the bible teaches that a man shall leave his father and mother and be one with his wife, we should be clear here that leaving your parents does not mean you should abandon them. The 'leave and cleave' means becoming independent in life – no longer depending on them for resources – emotional, financially, etc.

The most important person that should take this position apart from the Godhead, is your spouse. Couples should depend on each other and the Spirit of God for all resources and sustenance.

Your parents are still worthy of honour and each couple should ensure that their parents are duly honoured while they are alive.

A quick look into the dictionary shows that the word 'honour' connotes high regard with great respect and fulfilling an obligation or doing something morally right. With this in mind, we know that our parents must be highly regarded and treated with the highest level of respect, ensuring we fulfil our obligations to them, whatever this may be.

Most parents want the best for their children, and couples can still gain the benefit of the wisdom and counsel of their parents when they seek their advice. Couples should however, seek each other's permission before presenting matters to any set of parents.

Saying this, we have seen instances where some parents

will not want to 'break the parental ties' and this may result in different means of manipulation and control of one or both of the spouses. This is a sensitive area, but the couple must work together and stand strong to avoid this. They must be assertive in ensuring that the parents know that they are only seeking joint advice and the decision still remains with them.

Any parental advice or influence that puts a couple at odds with each other should be seriously considered for rejection, and such a source of advice needs to be avoided at all costs and all times. Couples should understand that they are now one indivisible unit, as we see from the marriage vows, 'what God has joined together, let no one separate...' It is the couple's task to identify sources of separation and jointly work to avoid them – even if the source is from a parent.

Staying together as a team should be an objective pursued without fear or favour with the help of the Holy Spirit.

10

CHILDREN

A heritage, a reward – keep it that way!

Psalm 127:3-5 (NIV)

*³ Children are a heritage from the Lord,
Offspring a reward from him.
⁴ Like arrows in the hands of a warrior
are children born in one's youth.
⁵ Blessed is the man
whose quiver is full of them.
They will not be put to shame
when they contend with their opponents in court.*

The first thing we need to know about children is that they are from God, and He has blessed us with them as a heritage and a reward. We should also note that children should be prayed for, from requesting and asking God for them, to raising them in a godly way till they leave you and form their own home. Learn to create a spiritual atmosphere around your children by constantly handing them over to God who already has the plans and purposes for their lives. Remember, every child is born innocent, though with the Adamic nature. What a child becomes in the next few years of their life will be as a result of your input – we don't have any excuse about that.

There has been a recent spate of stabbings and killings in the city of London where I currently pastor. These murders are committed by young boys in gangs with a drug culture. These young teenagers were once innocent and brought untold joy to their parents, but what went wrong? We can undoubtedly trace most of what went wrong in their lives to parental and home issues.

Children came as a blank board and we as parents were the first people to start writing on the tablets of their hearts with our words and actions. With that, they begin to join the dots and form their own opinions as they grow and mix with others (good, bad and ugly) who also contribute their own quota to the hearts of these impressionable young ones.

We must see each child God blesses us with as a unique God-project, and we should see ourselves as project managers who have to deliver the project to God; be it when we hand our daughters to the priest (representing God) to hand to their chosen husband, or receive a wife for our son in the presence of God. This is the day I call 'go-live' date – borrowing a project management term. Everything you have ever contributed to that child will now have to be used to raise their own home.

The child project is not an easy assignment for parents, and parents should always handle it with the seriousness it deserves, knowing, they are the next generation. Parents should recognise that their child becomes an extension of them in the society. I am sure no parent wants their child to become a liability to the society.

The Child to Maturity story:

Children, children, children! They change and impact everything as the Lord blesses each couple with them. I deliberately put this chapter toward the end; as everything that I have previously discussed tends to be impacted one way or the other with the arrival of the first child and in some cases, twins.

During courtship, couples find lots of time to be with each other and spend time together, and this continues till marriage and living together. Before that first child, it was easy to take decisions on a whim – you may both decide to jet out for a weekend without giving much considerations to other adults around you. You can both spend on each other lavishly and to the extent to which you have budgeted. Friends and family are considered as at and when the time permits, and when you both agree you are free. You may both even be satisfied with a motor-bike to get around, since it's only the two of you. How about tidying up and making the house as 'we want it'? Low maintenance! Anybody can come in any time, and the house will be picture perfect – just as you left it.

All these things change consciously or unconsciously once the first child arrives. Family, friends and well-wishers start their pilgrimage to your home, each bearing their gifts – useful or otherwise. Then there are the sleepless nights, and the increased costs of looking after the bundle of joy that God has delivered to you because He is pleased with you – 'a reward from him…' as the Psalmist calls it. The ample time you used to have with your spouse begins to reduce, not because you don't want to have this wonderful time together, but your baby has to have his or her own share of your time and can I mention here now, their demand for time may not be as you expected.

How about the emergency days? Baby all of a sudden running a temperature – well that can take you five hours at the hospital's Accident and Emergency unit

(A&E), and you are blessed if your visit is only once that week. You may have been sent home by a doctor who feels you were just fussing for nothing and it's only the weather. "Give the baby Calpol (Analgesic syrup) and that should be fine." Well, after a day or so, you notice the temperature is getting worse and not coming down, and there's the repeat journey to A&E again, only to now be told it's an infection and the baby is admitted and put on saline and antibiotics for about 4 days. Unplanned, unrehearsed, emergency time. This is a true story, and actually happened to us on a Christmas Day – and there was the turkey, well stuffed and abandoned.

This is not to scare anyone, but to bring the practicality of young married life home.

The cost of nappies, feeding, clothes, and toys soon begin to add up. Why am I saying this? TO MAKE SURE YOU TALK AND PLAN ABOUT CHILDREN BEFORE EMBARKING ON THAT JOURNEY.

Planning for your children before they even arrive, reduces the pressure that most couples who have not planned face.

I should add here, however, that the joy that comes from raising a child or children cannot be overemphasised.

The baby you were changing nappies for and bathing and rocking to sleep soon grows out of your rocking hands and into the freedom of the environment where exploration and learning starts. All your neatly arranged magazines, CDs, etcetera start coming down from the racks. Nothing is neat anymore. You spread learning mats, but that soon becomes limiting, and further exploration to other parts of the house starts. Before long, the crawling becomes walking, and walking soon turns to running and at that point you can afford not to not renew your gym membership as the exercise from the run around an active child gives you soon begin to take its toll. Tiredness sets in and you start looking for your bed at the earliest possible opportunity once your baby has fallen asleep.

Mostly, mothers take the brunt of all this, and this is where some men start feeling the 'blues of neglect.' The time they used to have with their wife has all but totally gone – they now feel as if they are now feeding on scrap time. If care is not taken, an average man may take the wrong decision on how to handle that phase. Some may just end up finding more time with friends and hobbies. As much as this may help a little, I feel it is counter productive to the future of the relationship. My suggestion to most is to embrace that phase together with their wife. Rather than leaving work and heading out with friends to the pub for socials, husbands should see it as an opportunity to get home early and help their wife or vice versa.

CHILDREN

Coming home early and helping your spouse to grab some rest while you also bond with your child is a win-win for you both and for your relationship. This is the time you must not let your need override your duties and responsibilities in the building of a godly home. Trust me this phase can determine the success of the next phase. Before you know it, that baby is now a child ready for nursery school.

The search for the best nursery, best minder or au-pair to do pick up runs if both parents are working will need prayerful consideration. If you wonder what has prayer got to do with it? Maybe, you revisiting the movie 'The hands that rocks the cradle' will help. Prayer is required at every step of development of your child.

We were blessed when our first child was growing up. We prayed for someone to look after her as we both were working parents, and God gave us a young Italian lady who wanted to come to the UK to learn English and was seeking a young family. God connected us, and the rest as they say is history. It was truly a match from God; as we became a blessing to her she became a blessing to us. She stayed with us, went to university at our advice, and now she's an international tour operator manager, married with her own two children. We still speak to her regularly. God can link you with people that will become helpers of destiny for you – if only you ask Him.

Before long your baby becomes independent and before you know it, it's time for secondary school, the teenage years; and quickly, comes the time they will have to leave home to go to the university. Between all these phases there are discussions and planning that need to be done. From how to discipline your children to how much independence you should accord them at each phase of growth. Trust me, all these things are important, and couples should consciously talk about them, so that what you assume is the right way of training your child may not become an issue with your spouse. I will always emphasise communication at all levels and phases of life.

Love must be the key to raising your children, but we should also remember that the bible teaches that God disciplines those He loves. So we should always note that discipline is a part of love as well. The style of discipline is what each family should decide and be sure it's within the biblical guidance and the laws of the land.

The following are a few important pointers I picked up while counselling which I feel every couple should be aware of when children are brought into the family dynamics:

> - **Neglect:** Be conscious to know that the lack of time with each other can lead to neglect of your spouse. Always remember, without your spouse there would not have been the child, so, consciously think of your spouse, and both of you should make time to be together. It may not be as regular as it used to be before, but talk about it and make time. If it was a daily set out time before, it may have to become weekly, but keep to it. It's good for not only both of you, but more importantly your child's development – as your child will grow up in a loving home where parents are not always bickering and arguing due to pressure and tension some of which comes from neglect and abandonment of each other.

- **Negatives:** Reduced time to be together may sometimes bring 'the negatives' – tensions, mistakes, errors, forgetfulness of important dates or times etc. It's not that they were not there before, but it may become more pronounced. Each spouse should make conscious effort to understand the situation and with a heart of 'first love' help the other spouse. It is not the time to start accentuating weaknesses and mistakes, you will only make things worse. Love, they say, covers a multitude of sins. This should be a key verse to operate by. It's so easy to spot an opportunity through your spouse's error or mistake to start spewing out all you have stored in your heart against your spouse.

This in itself is unforgiveness and bitterness of heart. You have the opportunity to 'crucify' your spouse for their mistake and you take it. You must repent from this spirit of selfishness and strife, knowing that where there is strife there's always all manner of evil works. As I say to many a counselee, the devil doesn't need a door into your home. He only needs a crack, and he will work on that crack to create a highway; and you know what his assignment is – to kill, steal and destroy. Don't be the spouse that will give the enemy an inroad into your home through the crack of unforgiveness, bitterness, jealousy, strife, and the list goes on... Be kind hearted towards one another – this is the key to dealing with negatives.

Always remember that you are married to each other and NOT to your children. One day the children will leave to build their own homes. DON'T allow your children to come between what God has joined together. It may not be easy but with a deliberate effort and practice, as a couple you can work towards ensuring that you give each other adequate attention without letting the children come between you.

11
THE FINAL C- THE CHALLENGE
God Will Do A New Thing

This is not just the conclusion but a challenge to Commitment to making your relationship, family and home an expression of God's heart for a godly union. Where God is concerned, He's always ready to begin with us again – He's always ready to do a new thing (Isaiah 43:19) with us – if only we allow Him.

For you to have read up to this point, I believe you are already in the category of people who want God to make a change in your situation or the situation of a loved one. I can assure you that God is able to make a way in the wilderness for relationships in combats and confusion. He is also able to create rivers in the desert for relationships going through dryness, deceit and decay.

We must trust God and His Word. If He says He can, then He can and He will - He can turn our wilderness into a great plantation and cause us to thrive in our relationships, families and homes.

Lastly, let me remind you of why this book was written again. I mentioned it at the beginning – God wanted me to write it to remind His children that challenges in relationships are hindering them from taking their place of purpose and stopping them from accomplishing for the Kingdom. Please always bear in mind that the purpose is to accomplish for God, and your relationship is an integral part of your 'tool-set' to help you accomplish – so handle it right.

Prayer

Father, I thank you for your dear children that you have led to read this book in pursuit of a godly insight and solution to the challenges of relationship. Lord I pray that you will lead them to the path of your solution. Grant them wisdom to work things out amicably with their spouses and help them to walk in abundance of your grace to ensure that only your will, counsel and purpose is accomplished in their lives and their relationships on a daily basis. That your name will continually be glorified in their lives and homes in Jesus name.

The Bible says, we should not be 'unaware of the devil's devices' – Father, we pray that every form of satanic operation and devices affecting the lives and relationships of your children, or any demonic altars (generational or otherwise) speaking against their lives and relationships be destroyed by the Power of the Holy Spirit in Jesus name.

Father, keep your children strong and focused on You and Your Word, let their spiritual eyes be open to see that they are not alone but you and the host of heaven are with them – let them also see what you are about to do and cause them to rise in faith and in strength to work with you to claim their relationship back for God's purpose in Jesus name.

We declare and proclaim victory in every area of their relationship and homes in Jesus name and by the power of the Holy Spirit. Amen.

Go and Prosper.

References

Aristotle, On the Soul, 350 B.C.E

New International Version, 1984

New Living Translation Bible, 1996

King James Version, 1982

Jean-Paul Sartre, "Freedom is what you do with what's been done to you."

Merriam-Webster's Dictionary of English Usage, 1974

Oxford English Dictionary, 2nd Edition, OUP 1989

Human Competition, Muse, 2019

Money Magazine, '2014 Survey of Couples and Money' < http://time.com/money/2800576/love-money-by-the-> 2019

Lorraine Harvey, 'As 'Divorce Day' Looms, Money Worries Top List of Reasons Why Married Couples Will Split in 2018' (2018) < https://www.slatergordon.co.uk/media-centre/press-releases/2018/01/as-divorce-day-looms-money-worries-top-list-of-reasons-why-married-couples-will-split-in-2018/> 2019

Dave Ramsey, 'Money, Marriage, and Communication' (2018) https://www.daveramsey.com/research/money-marriage-communication> accessed mm/2019

Alessandra Martelli, https://alessandramartelli.com/en/freebies/characteristics-effective-communication/2020

https://www.searchquotes.com/search/Unhealthy_Competition/#ixzz6bbl9Hbou